LIVERPOOL EVERYMAN AND PLAYHOUSE PRESENT
THE WORLD PREMIÈRE OF

UNPROTECTED

BY ESTHER WILSON, JOHN FAY, TONY GREEN AND LIZZIE NUNNERY

DIRECTED BY NINA RAINE

LIVERPOOL EVERYMAN AND PLAYHOUSE

About the Theatres

In 2000, two great regional reps were merged into a single company. At the beginning of 2004, buoyed up by Liverpool's impending status as European Capital of Culture in 2008, they entered a new and dynamic era. By returning to producing on a major scale, the Everyman and Playhouse have reclaimed their place on the national stage and generated an energy that has attracted acclaim, awards and audience loyalty.

The Liverpool Everyman and Playhouse theatres are always looking to bring the people of Merseyside a rich and varied portrait of the theatrical landscape. We have a strong and passionate commitment to new writing. Today's playwrights are tomorrow's theatrical legacy.

Unprotected is a unique piece. It is the result of months of research and the collaboration of a group of Liverpool writers, their director, these theatres and the people whose stories are told. It has a Liverpool voice but asks a question of any civilised society. It is very much of its time but its subject matter will be here tomorrow in this and any city, anywhere. Specific voices were captured; specific lives were lost but it is our hope that this play will make what was considered unworthy of note, matter.

Liverpool Everyman and Playhouse would like to thank all our current supporters:

Corporate Members A C Robinson and Associates, Benson Signs, Brabners Chaffe Street, C3 Imaging, Chadwick Chartered Accountants, Downtown Liverpool in Business, Duncan Sheard Glass, DWF Solicitors, EEF NorthWest, Grant Thornton, Hope Street Hotel, John Lewis, Mando Group, Morgenrot Chevaliers, Nonconform Design, Nviron Ltd, Synergy Colour Printing, The Mersey Partnership Victor Huglin Carpets.

Trusts & Grant-Making Bodies BBC Northern Exposure, BBC Radio Merseyside, The Eleanor Rathbone Charitable Trust, Five, The Harry Pilkington Trust, The Golsoncott Foundation,The Granada Foundation, Liverpool Culture Company, The Lynn Foundation, PH Holt Charitable Trust, The Pilkington General Fund, The Rex Makin Charitable Trust.

This theatre has the support of the Pearson Playwrights' Scheme sponsored by Pearson plc. Assisted by Business in the Arts: North West

Individual Supporters Peter and Geraldine Bounds, George C Carver, Councillor Eddie Clein, Mr and Mrs Dan Hugo, A. Thomas Jackson, Ms D Leach, Frank D Paterson, Les Read, Sheena Streather, Frank D Thompson, DB Williams and all those who prefer to remain anonymous.

Liverpool Everyman and Playhouse is a registered charity no, 1081229
www.everymanplayhouse.com

NEW WRITING AT THE LIVERPOOL EVERYMAN AND PLAYHOUSE

"A remarkable renaissance"
(Liverpool Daily Post)

As well as a major expansion in production the Theatres' revival is driven by a passionate commitment to new writing. *Unprotected* is the latest in a rich and varied slate of world, European or regional premières which has been enthusiastically received by Merseyside audiences and helped to put Liverpool's theatre back on the national map.

"Lyrical, muscular, full of indignation and compassion"
(The Sunday Times on *Yellowman*)

Highly acclaimed productions have included the European première of *Yellowman* by Dael Orlandersmith which transferred to Hampstead Theatre and successfully toured nationally, and regional premières of Conor McPherson's *Port Authority* and Simon Block's *Chimps*. And in just over two years, the theatres will have produced six world premières - *Fly* by Katie Douglas; *The Kindness of Strangers* by Tony Green; *Urban Legend* by Laurence Wilson; *The Morris* by Helen Blakeman; Gregory Burke's *On Tour* - (a co-production with London's Royal Court); *Unprotected* by Esther Wilson, John Fay, Tony Green, Lizzie Nunnery and *Paradise Bound* by Jonathan Larkin.

"The Everyman could wish for no finer 40th anniversary present than a return to form"
(The Guardian on *The Kindness of Strangers*)

Around the main production programme, the theatres run a range of projects and activities to create opportunities and offer support to writers at every career stage.

The commissioning programme invests in the creation of new work for both the Everyman and the Playhouse stages.

The Henry Cotton Writers on Attachment scheme is providing three young Liverpool writers with an intensive programme of creative and career development. Thanks to Five and to Pearson TV both Laurence Wilson and Tony Green recently benefited from year-long residencies. And an annual new writing festival, *Everyword*, offers a busy and popular week of seminars, sofa talks and work-in-progress readings.

"Laurence Wilson is another name to add to the theatre's long and glorious reputation for nurturing new talent"
(Liverpool Echo on *Urban Legend*)

The full programme at the Everyman and Playhouse blends this new work with bold interpretations of classic drama, and mixes our own Made in Liverpool productions with carefully hand-picked touring shows. By doing so, we aim to offer the people of Merseyside a rich and satisfying theatrical diet. But if we are driven by one thing more than all others, it is the conviction that an investment in new writing is an investment in our theatrical future.

For more information about the Everyman and Playhouse - including the full programme, off-stage activities such as playwright support, and ways in which you can support our investment in talent - visit www.everymanplayhouse.com.

CREDITS

THE COMPANY

Writers
Esther Wilson, John Fay,
Tony Green & Lizzie Nunnery

Director & Dramaturg
Nina Raine

Designer
Miriam Buether

Lighting Designer
Colin Grenfell

Sound Designer
Jason Barnes

Video & Projection Design
The Gray Circle

Video & Projection Assistant
Mandeep Ahira

Costume Supervisor
Jackie Orton

Casting Advisor
Lisa Makin

Production Manager
Emma Wright

Stage Manager
Sarah Lewis

Deputy Stage Manager
Roxanne Vella

Assistant Stage Manager
Louise Martin

Lighting Operators
Sean Pritchard, Mary Cummings

Stage Crew
Lindsey Bell, Paul McDonagh

Set Construction
Sam Kent, Howard Macaulay

Dramaturg
Suzanne Bell

Transcribers
Kathleen Fitzpatrick, Rebecca Sharpe,
Dan Wilson, Michael Gunwhy,
Lizzie Nunnery, Suzanne Bell

CAST

LEANNE BEST
ALI

NEIL CAPLE
COLIN/JOHN/BRIAN/LEE/
GOVERNMENT OFFICIAL

Leanne's theatre credits include:
34 (Fecund Theatre Company); *The Morris* and *Macbeth* (Liverpool Everyman); *Solitary Confinement* (King's Head Theatre); *Popcorn* (Liverpool Playhouse); *Julius Caesar, Nicholas Nickleby, Live Like Pigs, Our Country's Good, Platanov, Macbeth* and *The Crucible* (LIPA).

Television includes: *Casualty, Heatwave, Wire in the Blood, Memory of Water* and *Casbah - A Documentary.*

Radio includes: *The Importance of Being Earnest.*

Leanne has also participated in rehearsed readings and workshops for new writing at the Liverpool Everyman's *Everyword* festival, the Actor's Centre and the Young Vic.

Neil's theatre credits include:
Othello (Tokyo Globe); *The Merry Wives of Windsor, The Wind In The Willows* and *The Trackers of Oxyrynchus* (National Theatre); *A Comedy of Errors* and *Macbeth* (Royal Shakespeare Company).

Television credits include:
Brookside, Cadfael and *The Bullion Boys.*

CAST

PAULINE DANIELS
PAT/JILL

Pauline's theatre credits include:
Liverpool Heartbeats, And The Beat Goes On and *Elsie and Norm's Macbeth* (Liverpool Everyman); *Misery* (The Brindley, Runcorn); *Snow White* (Floral Pavilion Theatre, New Brighton); *Twopence To Cross The Mersey* (Liverpool Empire); *Breezeblock Park, Oliver Twist, Billy Liar, Gypsy* and *Chicago* (Liverpool Playhouse); *A Saint She Ain't* (King's Head/ Apollo Theatre) and *Shirley Valentine* (Touring, Liverpool Playhouse and Liverpool Everyman).

Television includes: *The Street/ The Likes Of Us, Liverpool 1* and *Brookside.*

Radio includes: Presenter of BBC Radio Merseyside's *Morning Breakfast Show.*

PAUL DUCKWORTH
ANDY/BILLY/STEPHEN/KEVIN

Paul's theatre credits include:
Urban Legend (Liverpool Everyman); *You Are Here* (Unity Theatre); *Golden Boy, Man Who Stole a Winter Coat* and *The Corrupted Angel* (national tours with Base Chorus Company, including the Royal Opera House); *Slappers and Slapheads* (Royal Court and Empire Theatres, Liverpool and the Opera House, Manchester); *River Fever* (Unity Theatre); *Moving Voices* (Sheffield Crucible); *The Man Who Cracked, Backwater* (national tour - Spike Theatre Company) and *Madam I'm Adam* (Edinburgh Festival 2005 - Spike Theatre Company).

Television credits include:
Brookside and *The Courtroom.*

Film credits include: *Backbeat* and *Ward 15.*

CAST

TRICIA KELLY
TRINA/CATHERINE/LUCY/MARCIA

Tricia's theatre credits include:
The Maths Tutor (Hampstead Theatre);
Some Explicit Polaroids (Out Of Joint
tour); *Jamaica Inn, Barbarians*
and *Dancing At Lughnasa* (Salisbury
Playhouse); *King Lear* (West
Yorkshire Playhouse and Hackney
Empire); *Two* (West Yorkshire
Playhouse); *Ion* and *Julius Caesar*
(Royal Shakespeare Company);
*Much Ado About Nothing, As You
Like It* and *The Seagull* (Sheffield
Crucible); *The Last Supper, Seven
Lears* and *Victory* (The Wrestling
School); *Fen, Deadlines* and *A
Mouthful Of Birds* (Joint Stock); *Fen*
(New York); *Beauty And The Beast*
(Liverpool Playhouse) and *Freedom
Of The City* (Liverpool Everyman).

Television credits include: *Casualty,
The Bill, My Family, Dangerous Lady*
and *In Sickness And In Health.*

Film credits include: *Top Dog, Big
Feet* and *A Small Dance.*

JOAN KEMPSON
DIANE/JENNI

Joan's theatre credits include:
Iron (Manchester Evening News
Best Production 2005) and *What's
In The Cat* (Contact Theatre,
Manchester); *Rutherford and Son*
(Manchester Royal Exchange Theatre);
*Beyond Belief: The Harold Shipman
Report* (Library Theatre, Manchester);
Grannies (Penny Plain Theatre) and
Marigold (Dukes Theatre, Manchester).

Television credits include: *Doctors,
The Bill, Early Doors* (Smile Best
Comedic Performance Award for
entire cast), *King Of Fridges, Clocking
Off (1, 2, 3 & 4), Having It Off, Stan
The Man, Coronation Street (regular),
North Square, Always and Everyone,
Children's Ward, City Central,
Dockers, My Wonderful Life* and
The Cops.

Radio credits include: *Ralphie
Stanze's Jail Diaries* and *Rain
On The Just.*

COMPANY

JOHN FAY WRITER

Greatly committed to the theatre, John was a founder member of Kirkby Response. He has received commissions from Paines Plough to write *Waste*, which went on tour to The West Yorkshire Playhouse, Newcastle, The Bristol Old Vic and The Bolton Octagon; and for his full-length play *Eat My Eyes*. John's stage plays include *The Dream Of Joe Hill; A Grave Mistake; Hammer In The Hand* and *Deadfish & Chipboard*.

John has written for many top-rated television Drama Series, including *Brookside, Clocking Off* and *Coronation Street*. His episode from 2003, "Richard Hillman's murder confession", garnered over 19 million viewers - the highest audience for television drama anywhere in the world that year.

John is developing with his brother, Steven, a drama series for Mersey TV; has written two episodes of *Blue Murder* and is currently working on *Mobile*, a three-part thriller, for Granada TV.

John's full-length play, *The Cruel Sea*, is in development towards a community prouction in 2007 at the Everyman.

TONY GREEN WRITER

Tony graduated from David Edgar's MA in Playwriting Studies at Birmingham University in 1998. He became an associate writer of the Liverpool Everyman and Playhouse in 2001, and was Writer on Attachment in 2002 when he first began work on *The Kindness of Strangers* which was staged at the Everyman in 2004.

His previous stage work includes, *Permanent Damage* at the Unity Theatre, Liverpool - produced by Liverpool Lunchtime Theatre, 1996; (the same play received separate productions at The Questor's Theatre and The Man in the Moon Theatre, London, in the same year); *Audrey* - rehearsed public reading - directed by Max Stafford-Clark at the Soho Theatre, London (2001).

He has also written for radio, *It's A Wonderful Divorce* (Radio 4, 2001) and has made a short film, *Run Piglet Run!* (winner of the North West Vision Digi Shorts competition, 2004).

He was the Theatres' FiveArts Cities Writer in Residence (2004/05) and is working on another stage commission for the Everyman and Playhouse, *Curfew.*

COMPANY

LIZZIE NUNNERY WRITER

Lizzie Nunnery's first play *The Fine Art of Falling to Pieces*, was one of the winners of the Oxford Student New Writing Competition, 2003. It was given a student production at the Moser Theatre, Oxford, and a two week run at the Zoo Theatre, Edinburgh. On returning to Liverpool she joined the Everyman Young Writers Group through which her first dramaturged play, *Love*, was read as part of the 2004 Everyword Festival. Her one act play, *Dragon Fruit*, was given rehearsed readings at Soho Theatre and the Liverpool Everyman in March 2005 and June 2005 respectively. Lizzie also worked as a shadow writer last July, on BBC Radio 4's forthcoming thriller series, *Lost in Liverpool*, and is currently developing a new full length stage play as Henry Cotton Writer on Attachment at the Liverpool Everyman and Playhouse. She has recently been selected as one of fifty writers to take part in a nationwide development scheme in connection with the BBC and the Royal Court Theatre, London.

ESTHER WILSON WRITER

Esther's play *My Eyes…Your Smile?* has received readings at the West Yorkshire Playhouse and at the Liverpool Everyman *Everyword* Festival 2004.

Theatre credits include: Community Arts work projects, *Positive Acts and Direct Action* (Liverpool Everyman Theatre) and *Our Town* (Merseyside Dance Initiative/The Millennium Dome); *SoulSkin* (Red Ladder Theatre Company and national touring production) and *Noah's Ark* with Lee Beagley (Walk the Plank Commission, National Tour). She has also written *T.I.E Healthy Arts Initiative*, *Rollercoaster* and *Whirlwind*.

Radio credits include: *Hiding Leonard Cohen* and *Hush Little Baby* (BBC Radio 4).

Awards include: 2002 Winner of BBC's Northern Exposure Competition (Short film category); *The Swimming Man*. 2004 Winner of Mental Health in the Media Award for BBC Radio 4 play *Hiding Leonard Cohen*.

NINA RAINE DIRECTOR

Nina graduated from Christ Church Oxford with a double First in English Literature. In April 2000 she won the Channel Four/Jerwood Spaces Young Regional Theatre Director bursary and began as a Trainee Director at the Royal Court Theatre in July 2000. She has recently completed a commission for Hampstead Theatre and her first play *Rabbit* was shortlisted for the Verity Bargate Award 2004. *Rabbit* will be staged at the Old Red Lion Theatre in May 2006.

Theatre credits as Director include: *Vermillion Dream* (Salisbury Playhouse) and *Eskimo Sisters* (Southwark Playhouse).

Further credits: *Henry V* (as Staff Director - National Theatre) and *The Holy Terror* (as Associate Director - West End).

As Assistant Director: *Fucking Games, Ashes to Ashes, Mountain Language, Mouth to Mouth, Far Away* and *My Zinc Bed* (Royal Court Theatre) and *Presence* (Theatre Upstairs, Royal Court Theatre).

MIRIAM BUETHER DESIGNER

Miriam trained in costume design at Akademie für Kostüm Design, Hamburg. She was the overall winner of the 1999 Linbury Prize.

Theatre credits include: *Trade* (RSC, Soho Theatre); *After the End* (Traverse Theatre, tour Berlin); *Way to Heaven* (Royal Court); *Platform* (ICA); *The Wonderful World of Dissocia* (Lyceum Edinburgh, Tron Glasgow - Critics Award for Theatre in Scotland 2005); *Guantanamo* (Tricycle Theatre, West End, New York and San Francisco); *The Dumb Waiter* and *Other Pieces* (Oxford Playhouse); *People Next Door* (Traverse Theatre and tour New York); *Red Demon* (Young Vic and tour Japan); *Bintou* (Arcola Theatre); *Eskimo Sisters* (Southwark Playhouse) and *Lebensspiele* (Three Mills Island Studios).

Dance credits: *TooT* and *Possibly Six* (Grands Ballets de Canadiens, Montreal); *Outsight* and *Tender Hooks* (Foundation Gulbenkian, Lisbon); *Track* (Scottish Dance Theatre); *Body Of Poetry* (Komische Oper, Berlin, Lisbon and tour); and *7DS* (Rambert Dance Company, Sadlers Wells).

Opera credits: *The Death of Klinghoffer* (Scottish Opera and Edinburgh International Festival).

COMPANY

COLIN GRENFELL
LIGHTING DESIGNER

Colin regularly lights productions for Improbable Theatre, including *Theatre Of Blood* at the National Theatre last summer and *The Hanging Man* which premiered at the West Yorkshire Playhouse in May 2003 before touring the UK and abroad. Other work for them includes their 2001 show at the Royal Court *Upstairs*, *Spirit* and the UK and US hit, *Lifegame*, as well as the multi-award-winning *70 Hill Lane*.

Recent stage credits include: *Aladdin And The Enchanted Lamp* (Bristol Old Vic); *Presence* (Theatre Royal, Plymouth); *Spirit* (Theatre Workshop, New York); *Travels With My Virginity* (Battersea Arts Centre); *Eugene Onegin and Andrea Chenier* (Holland Park Opera); *Tick Tick… Boom!* (Menier Chocolate Factory); *Bye Bye Birdie* (Guildhall School of Music and Drama); *Falstaff* (RSAMD); *Old King Cole* (Unicorn Theatre at the Cochrane); *La Bohème* (English Touring Opera); *The Unthinkable* (Crucible Theatre Sheffield); *Kes* (Manchester Royal Exchange); *Marie Luise* (The Gate Theatre); *Lifegame* (National Theatre); *The Rape of Lucretia* (The Guildhall School of Music and Drama) and *The Marriage of Figaro* (RSAMD).

JASON BARNES
SOUND DESIGNER

Jason is Head of Sound at Bristol Old Vic.

Bristol Old Vic credits include:
The Barber of Seville, Air Guitar, Aladdin and the Enchanted Lamp, Tamburlaine (Bristol, the Barbican); *The Importance of Being Earnest, The Turn of the Screw, The Odyssey* (Bristol, Liverpool and West Yorkshire Playhouse); *Two's Company* and *Child of the Snow, Alice's Adventures in Wonderland, Twelfth Night, Arcadia, Killer Joe, Private Peaceful* (Bristol and tour); *Loot, Kangaroo Valley, Paradise Lost, Cinderella, True West, The Comedy of Errors, The Caretaker, A Midsummer Night's Dream, The Owl Who Was Afraid of the Dark, Les Liaisons Dangereuses, "Master Harold"… and the Boys, Mrs Warren's Profession, The Wizard of Oz, The Real Thing* (Bristol/tour); *Up the Feeder, Down the 'Mouth and Back Again, One Love* (Bristol/Lyric Hammersmith); *Look Back in Anger, A Streetcar Named Desire, Denial, A Busy Day* (Bristol/West End); *Blues Brother Soul Sister.*

Other theatre includes: *The Redcliffe Hermit* (Bristol Industrial Museum); *Dr Faustus* (Liverpool Playhouse); *Arms and the Man* (national tour); *Death and the Ploughman* (Gate Theatre); *The King of Prussia* and *Insignificance* (Chichester Festival Theatre) and *Earth and Sky* (Nuffield Theatre and tour).

THE GRAY CIRCLE
VIDEO AND PROJECTION DESIGN

The Gray Circle (David Newton, Andrew Savage, Yuri Tanaka, Thomas Gray) is a London-based moving image and projection design company with an international client base. Founded in 1998 by Thomas Gray, the company draws on collective talent to combine imagination with digital technology, creating moving imagery for performing arts and corporate communications.
www.thegraycircle.com

Current and upcoming projects include: *The Lord of the Rings* on stage, directed by Matthew Warchus, designed by Rob Howell, at the Princess of Wales Theatre, Toronto, Canada. *Dirty Dancing* by Eleanor Bergstein premiering Hamburg Germany and *Body Memories*, Ming-Shen Ku Dance, opening late 2006 Taipei, Taiwan.

Recent stage productions include: Wagner's *Twilight of the Gods* directed by Phyllida Lloyd, design by Richard Hudson (ENO, London); *3 Musketiere: Das Musical* (Theater des Westens, Berlin Germany); Philip Pullman's *His Dark Materials* (National Theatre, London) and the DV8 Physical Theatre productions; *Bound to Please* and *Happiest Day of My Life* (world tours).

COMPANY THANKS

Maurice Bessman and Bill Morrison
Malcolm Mellows and XCel Video
for their generosity
Keith Winstanley at Merseyside Police
Jackie Spent at The Brook Clinic
Fiona Lewis
Joanne Heffernan
Edge Hill Salvage
Daniel Dougan at 02 Phones
Merseytravel
WHISC
John Mealing from Propaganda
Howard Macaulay

STAFF

Vicky Adlard House Manager, **Laura Arends** Marketing Officer, **Deborah Aydon** Executive Director, Jane Baxter Box Office Manager, **Rob Beamer** Chief Electrician (Playhouse), **Lindsey Bell** Technician, Suzanne Bell Literary Manager, **Gemma Bodinetz** Artistic Director, **Emma Callan** Cleaning Staff, Moira Callaghan Theatre and Community Administrator, **Colin Carey** Security Officer, **Stephen Carl-Lokko** Security/Fire Officer, **Mary Cummings** Deputy Chief Technician, **Angela Dooley** Cleaning Staff, Allan Foy Assistant House Manager, **Roy Francis** Maintenance Technician, **Rosalind Gordon** Box Office Supervisor, **Mike Gray** Deputy Technical Stage Manager, **Helen Griffiths** Deputy House Manager, **Jayne Gross** Development Manager, **Stuart Holden** IT and Communications Manager, Alison Jones Interim General Manager, **Sarah Kelly** Stage Door/ Receptionist, **Sue Kelly** Cleaning Staff, **Steven Kennett** Assistant Maintenance Technician (Performance), **Sven Key** Fire Officer, **Lynn-Marie Kilgallon** Internal Courier, **Gavin Lamb** Marketing Assistant, **Rachel Littlewood** Community Outreach Co-ordinator, **Robert Longthorne** Building Development Director, **Leonie Mallows** Deputy Box Office Manager, **Ged Manson** Cleaning Staff, **Lucy McDougall** Finance Assistant, **Peter McKenna** Cleaning Staff, **Jason McQuaide** Technical Stage Manager (Playhouse), **Kirstin Mead** Development Officer, **Louise Merrin** Marketing Manager, **Brian Murphy** Bar Manager, **Paul Murray** Box Office Assistant, Liz Nolan Assistant to the Directors, **Lizzie Nunnery** Literary Assistant, **Sarah Ogle** Marketing Director, **Sue Parry** Theatres Manager, **Sean Pritchard** Chief Technician (Everyman), Collette Rawlinson Stage Door/Receptionist, **Victoria Rope** Programme Coordinator, **Rebecca Ross-Willams** Theatre and Community Director, **Jeff Salmon** Technical Director, **Steve Sheridan** Assistant Maintenance Technician, **Jackie Skinner** Education Co-ordinator, **Amy Smith** Box Office Assistant, **Louise Sutton** Box Office Assistant, **Jennifer Tallon–Cahill** Deputy Chief Electrician, **Pippa Taylor** Press and Media Officer, **Marie Thompson** Cleaning Supervisor/ Receptionist, **Hellen Turton** Security Officer, **Paul Turton** Finance Manager, **Deborah Williams** House Manager, **Laurence Wilson Pearson** Writer-in-Residence, **Emma Wright** Technical Manager.

Thanks to all our Front of House team and casual Box Office staff

Henry Cotton Writers on Attachment:
Jonathan Larkin, Michael McLean, Lizzie Nunnery

Board Members:
Cllr Warren Bradley, Professor Michael Brown (Chair), Mike Carran, Michelle Charters, Rod Holmes, Vince Killen, Professor E. Rex Makin, Andrew Moss, Roger Phillips, Sara Williams.

Company Registration No. 3802476 Registered Charity No. 1081229

Thanks to our Interact team:
Mickey Chandler, Vinnie Cleghorne, Yvonne Fogg, Patrick Graham, Kim Johnson, Chief Martin Okuboh, Helen Renner, Edward Terry, Eugene Weaver, Robert Weaver and Malique Jamal Al-Shabazz.

Interact is a voluntary group of people working to improve cultural diversity in our theatres as both audience members and employees. If you are interested in becoming a member of the Interact team or need more information please call the Marketing Department on: 0151 706 9106 or write to **Interact, Liverpool and Merseyside Theatres Trust, FREEPOST NATN48, Liverpool L1 3ZY.**

UNPROTECTED

by

Esther Wilson
John Fay
Tony Green
Lizzie Nunnery

JOSEF WEINBERGER PLAYS

LONDON

Dedicated to the memory of Hanane Parry, Pauline Stephen,
Anne Marie Foy

Thank you to everyone who has given their
time and stories to the making of this play.

The process of creating *Unprotected* started in January 2005. The Liverpool Everyman brought together five writers whose work had a strong social and political sensibility, to discuss a theme for a piece of verbatim theatre which would address an important and topical Liverpool issue. Lively debate followed, exploring issues of regeneration, Liverpool's place as European Capital of Culture, housing, capitalism, etc.

At this time, Liverpool City Council had just made a proposal for a managed zone for street sex workers, and it was universally decided that this issue, while specific, also encompassed many of these wider issues. Sex as a commodity is not something people want to talk about; they want to hide behind statistics and close their ears to the human story. Verbatim theatre enabled us to go to the heart of the issue, giving a voice to those most involved with and affected by street sex work. Esther Wilson was already researching sex workers for a radio piece so the timing seemed fortuitous. The creation of Unprotected began in earnest.

Each writer took a different group of people as their focus (residents, sex workers, police, politicians, punters, outreach workers), working tirelessly to source material, forge relationships and gain trust.

Tony Green took the difficult task of contacting punters, resorting to requests on chat pages and eventually even a classified ad before he gained two valuable and lucid sources. As a council member informed us, it was the appalling murder of Hanane Parry and Pauline Stephen, that had turned talk of a managed zone in to a very serious proposition. John Fay sourced the mothers of these murdered women and Esther began a series of meetings and interviews with street sex worker, "Ali".

For everyone who read or heard these interviews, it soon became clear that these women's stories constituted the human heart around which the political debate moved, leaving it indisputable that they should form the drive of the narrative. With the trust that was developing between writers and sources, many of whom were sharing intimate and sometimes harrowing stories for the first time, came a grave sense of responsibility.

As the taped interviews began to pour in, the task of transcribing was both an arduous and emotional process. Over 600 pages of transcripts were gathered. From this enormous body of testimony a coherent "play" which would be read at the Everyman in June had to be garnered. Nina Raine, a director with a strong background in new writing and a writer herself was chosen to direct the reading.

The evening was an electric experience; the debate following the play fuelled with such passion, that there was a consensus amongst all involved that one night was not enough for such important stories and for such a potent project.

A few months later a slightly smaller writing team: Esther Wilson, Tony Green, John Fay and Lizzie Nunnery, met again, hungry to push the piece further. They then embarked on the task of finding new sources and re-interviewing old ones, with an emphasis on filling the gaps in the stories, but also on finding the emotions and personalities behind some of the more formal and official figures; Lizzie Nunnery interviewing one political figure in her living room!

Nina Raine became a vital part of the process, conducting interviews alongside the writers and playing an intrinsic role in the research, editing and collating of material.

It was during this time, in September 2005, that Anne Marie Foy, a Liverpool street sex worker, was brutally murdered. This shocking reality brought the situation into startling focus, spurring all on to give this issue a voice that spoke louder than government wrangling and political-correctness. Between Christmas and New Year interviews in the press with Fiona McTaggart began to appear, implying that the government would be giving new directives on sex work, and in mid-January these directives were announced. There would be a general policy of zero tolerance on prostitution, and a no to managed zones. The writers needed to react to these announcements immediately, returning to sources and gathering new information: many of them keen to articulate their frustration.

With production dates looming, over 1000 pages of transcripts were brought together and distilled, through meetings with the writers, director and dramaturges, to a 60 page script on our stage. There were more moving stories, startling insights and gripping dramatic moments than could possibly be included, but all involved strived to arrive at a piece of theatre that did service to the gravity of the content, and to the Everyman Theatre's tradition of socio-political theatre, giving voice to stories at the heart of our community, and beyond.

Suzanne Bell
February 2006

CHARACTERS

THE MOTHERS

DIANE: 50s, working class. Typical 'mum.'
PAT: Mid-50s, strong, resilient woman. Chain smokes.

THE SEX WORKERS

ALI: Late 20s, skinny, attractive, 'edgy'.
MARCIA: 'Working girl', 40s.
DENNI: 'Working girl', 40s.
JILL: 'Working girl', 40s.

THE PUNTERS

STEPHEN: 40s. He's smartly dressed, wearing a very expensive suit, shirt, tie. His shoes are polished to perfection. Healthy complexion. Very clean. He's wearing expensive aftershave. He exudes self-confidence. And – just by looking at him – you just know he's got a bone-crunching handshake. He has a mobile phone with him.

BRIAN: Mid-40s, quite trim, fit, healthy. A security alarm fitter with his own business.

THE POLITICIAN

CATHERINE: Married woman in her fifties, hardworking, respectable, confident, forthright. She's wearing a smart blue dress-suit. She is carrying a stack of work folders.

THE POLICEMAN

KEVIN: A healthy, fit-looking man in his mid 40s. He's wearing a protective body vest.

THE OUTREACH WORKERS

LUCY: Late forties. She has short, dark, hair, sticking upwards chaotically. She is highly energetic; a constant performer. At intervals she sips a drink.

ANDY: Thirties, camp, 'Woolly-back' accent.
COLIN: Forties, camp, smartly dressed.

THE DRUGS WORKER

LEE: 40s, 'Scally' type. Wears an Everton top, with an Everton band around his wrist.

THE RESIDENTS

TRINA
JOHN

DOUBLING:

DIANE/DENNI: 50s
ALI: 20s
PAT/JILL: 50s
TRINA/CATHERINE/LUCY/MARCIA: 40s
BRIAN/LEE/COLIN: 40s
STEPHEN/KEVIN/BILLY/ANDY: 40s

ACT ONE

Scene One

The Drop In – Part One

ANDY *is taking piles of clothes out of bin bags and putting them onto chairs/floor.* COLIN *is setting out thermoses of soup and polystyrene cups, rolls in plastic bags, condoms in paper envelopes, etc, out on a table. A make-shift 'memorial'. Chocolates, Shepherds Pie, hot drinks, tarot cards depicting female archetypes and candles welcome the women.* ALI *comes in: mid thirties, skinny, attractive.*

ALI	Fucking freezing out there.
COLIN	Can I take your date of birth love?
ALI	20 June, 1977.
COLIN	(*as he writes it down*) You're early tonight, you're the first in. How's it going, any problems?
ALI	(*checking out the piles of clothes*) Yeah sound.
COLIN	Do you want to take part in our housing survey? It'll take two minutes.
ALI	Can I do it after?
COLIN	Okay, the doctor'll see you in a minute love.
ALI	(*inspecting candles, chocs, etc*) Oh, is this all for –
ANDY	Yeah. Wanna light a candle for her?
ALI	Fuckin 'ell! Gis' a minute.
	(*During the next exchange* ALI *is picking through the clothes, inspecting the pile of makeup, helping herself to soup, etc.*)

ANDY   (*gesturing to audience*) Have you heard about the project that these're doing?

ALI   (*in a mock St Helens accent*) No.

ANDY   Are you taking the piss out of my accent?

ALI   (*in same voice*) No love.

ANDY   Are yer interested?

ALI   No.

ANDY   (*laughing*) I didn't think ye would be.

ALI   (*in her own voice now*) What is it love?

ANDY   If I talk scouse will you talk to me?

ALI   Yeh. Go 'head. Alright then.

ANDY   They're doing a project about managed zones.

ALI   Yeh? So what happens?

ANDY   Well they're gonna get actors and actresses to portray your words.

ALI   And what do we get, like?

ANDY   Goody bags, what they brought today.

ALI   (*inspecting the pile of stuff*) Three lippy bits and a bracelet? That's crap! (*Coming forward.*) My face isn't gonna be on that is it? It's just using the voices, isn't it? Okay. That's cool. Alright. Cool. Cool.

(*Speaking to audience.*)

I don't think that a managed zone's any good because alright, it's legal in Amsterdam, but people are on holiday there, they're home here, de ye know what I mean? Like if anyone got murdered, say if they wanna vehicle

recognition – registration and all that – people
getting letters through the door. Now I
wouldn't want that if I was a family man, de ye
know what I mean?

I've worked down here for a long time now and
me meself I don't think it would personally
work. 'Cause I've spoke to a few punters about
it and they've said they wouldn't use it. And
then like yer in an enclosed area where there's
a lot of girls working. Ye know and one car
stops and one girl's gonna think it's for
another and the other one's gonna – it's gonna
cause a lot of trouble.

But if it could work it would be good for us –
for safety reasons. Because, erm, we do get
picked on and I don't think the police listen to
a lot of what happens to us.

(*She looks at the 'memorial'.*)

It's frightening but it's not the first murder to
happen is it? So it's just one of them things.
We know the risk we take when we go out so –
I go out again but what I mean is you're not
less scared or anything. You know the risks.

You know . . . and people don't believe this . . .
but we stop an awful lot of abuse in families.
Rape. Fellas going home, taking it out on their
wives for having a bad day. They'll go out and
they'll do something . . . you know, whatever?
Mad things with a prostitute, get rid of all that
stress and when they go home . . . to their
wives . . . they're whistling. Do you know what
I mean? And it could be these women residents
that hate us – their husbands could be doing it.
No one knows.

Scene Two

The residents have appeared – one man and one woman.

TRINA	I'll support this managed zone if it's away from residents . . .
JOHN	Not in a residential area.
TRINA	And it's not about NIMBY either. I've been accused of NIMBY. Not In My Back Yard. Well I don't think it should be in anyone's back yard. Two thousand residents I, erm, speak for, I represent, and I was elected properly, at a public meeting.
	We were here first. This is where we live. I've been brought up in this area. And I've got my parents there, worked all their lives, and now they're retired in a little bungalow that they love, and they're getting persecuted by prostitutes and kerb crawlers. Me mum's not confident, you know. We're all grown up and she's still saying 'Be careful'. 'Coz you never grow up, do you, in your parents' eyes?
JOHN	I'm just so glad I haven't got kids. It's really sad, I'm dead protective of my dogs. I mean if I had kids I'd be so worried I'd probably drive them to the point of distraction, know what I mean?
TRINA	I was worried about my daughter going to school. They were young at the time, you know, and they'd be saying, well what are they? What's prostitutes? You shouldn't have to educate your kids talking about prostitutes for God's sakes. Our theory is, with the Capital of Culture, they want this zone to be in the city centre, like a tourist attraction.
JOHN	And I think that's absolutely disgusting, and if you get that point over that would be great.
TRINA	My daughter was waiting on Shaw Street at the bus stop, and two prostitutes approached her. They were quite intimidating. They were asking

her for – you know to use her mobile phone and her lip gloss. She looks nothing like a prostitute. She's my daughter and she's a healthy looking young girl and she's not thin. She's got all her own teeth – she's got lovely teeth. You know them prostitutes are very gaunt-looking, the street prostitutes – they've got no teeth, they look undernourished. You can see who's a prostitute. But you don't speak to them.

JOHN   Two of my elderly residents said they had been basically approached by a prostitute, assaulted, grabbed and stopped. We have now got young children seeing open prostitution in the streets. Now, you know, call me a prude but it's not the way forward really is it?

TRINA   A young girl, she's – thirteen she was at the time – and a kerb-crawler come along and practically dragged her in. A driving instructor come to her aid. He'd seen it, thank God, and he got out his car and actually rescued the girl.

JOHN   I just feel like the kids in this area haven't got a chance, basically. (*He leaves.*)

TRINA   They're supposed to be doing a clampdown, but I've been trying to get them to do that for four years. We've actually got a tolerance zone at the moment because we're tolerating prostitution. (*Pause.*) Me personally I'd say, I will support this managed zone, but I'm not supporting it in our community. No way. We can't live a normal life. You're worried sick all the time from when your daughter or your son walks out the door. Plus you're worried yourself when you go out. You're looking over your shoulder all the time. Two murders in the area, which was just horrific. These were young women, you know, whatever some people say. Two young women who had severe drug addiction who were on the streets and got murdered . . . just shouldn't happen.

(*Lights start to come up on* PAT *and* DIANE.)

ALI   At the time I just stopped working. I was waiting to go into rehab, right? And through that, I ended up working again. Something like that comes along and hits yer like a ton of shit, the first thing yer onto, is drugs. 'Cos when things like that happen, it's like . . . yer head's gone, and you know, you think, that could be me.

TRINA   They were found like just along the road there, Netherfield Road. It was terrifying, y'know. Terrifying for us, and for them. Y'know, murderers around. That's what they attract though.

(TRINA *leaves.* DIANE *has come forward.*)

DIANE   I was ironing. We were going to Scotland. And, erm, I hate Scotland now, hate it. And then this bombshell comes. I seen these two fellas in suits pull up between me and next door, and I thought – they could be anybody, couldn't they? But I knew they were police, and I knew they were coming to tell me about Hanane. They were looking for Pauline, the other girl. But nobody reported Hanane missing. She'd been dead for like nine days. The body was decomposed, and chopped into pieces, and half of it was taken to Stanley Park, and the other half dumped in bin bags. They didn't know her name. They didn't know who she was. They knew she was mixed race. That's all they knew about her.

Scene Three

PAT *is sitting at her dining table smoking a cigarette. She's in her late 50s. A strong, resilient woman – a survivor who's seen more than her fair share of tragedy. She has a chunky white cardigan draped over her shoulders because she's sat*

*near to the patio glass door and it's open slightly. It's open
because she's a chain-smoker. She doesn't like the smell of
cigarettes in her well-kept room. (And probably because she
has a couple of guests.)*

*On a small table stands an electric fresh air machine which,
periodically, emits an audible waft of scented fragrance.*

Off to one side a sofa/armchair with a folded up Daily Mirror
resting on the arm.

*The patio looks onto a well-kept garden. And, because the
door is open slightly, we can hear the rain outside. A steady
downpour, but not too heavy.*

BILLY *enters with a mug of tea. He places it down on the table,
affectionately rubs* PAT's *shoulder, she touches his hand. He
returns to his place on the sofa/chair where he resumes
reading the* Daily Mirror. *(NB: Although he's reading the
paper,* BILLY'S *always listening to what* PAT *is saying. He
seldom looks over but he registers everything.)*

PAT   From the day she was born she did nothin' but
            cry. She was just one of them babies. A real
            crier. I asked the nurse in the hospital what was
            wrong with her . . . she said, "Oh, she's just
            one of them kids." A very unhappy baby. She
            cried when I picked her up and she cried when I
            put her down. I couldn't understand why this
            child came in to the world screamin' . . . and
            never stopped. She never stopped crying until
            she was thirteen. She was a horrible child.
            (*Beat. She laughs at what she's just said – an
            affectionate laugh.*) Horrible child.

            (*We see that* DIANE *is sitting, too. She has a
            black and white anti-racism rubber band on
            her wrist. There is a phone on a small table
            nearby. A pile of photographs on the floor
            which* DIANE *occasionally refers to.*)

DIANE   Oh she was lovely. She stuttered from when
            she first started speaking, but, oh, she was
            lovely. Her dad was a lab technician. When she

was ten months old, he said "I'm going home and I'm gonna get a passport so I can come back and live here." But all this time . . . when all this was going on . . . uh . . . that policewoman – what's her name? – had been shot in London. So they withdrew all contact, didn't they? With Libya, which is where he's from. So he said he found it very hard to get, uhm, a visa to come back. I'll never know. I think he was married over there, but I'll never know. I think he chose his family over there. She always wanted to know what her dad . . . who her dad was, where he come from and everything. She wanted to see a photograph of him. First thing she said was, "God, look at his hair!". 'Coz she ended up with hair that was Afro hair and she wouldn't go to the front door or the back door with her hair down because people would say that she was a Paki. So she never wore her hair down, ever.

PAT

Pauline loved her hair. Her hair was down to her bum. It was her crowning glory as they say. But she was manic over it. (*She takes a long drag on her cigarette.*) She didn't know what she wanted in life. She kept sayin' "All I want is a baby. That's all I want, I want a baby to love." This is when she was thirteen. She sat on the bed cryin' . . . "What am I gonna do with me life, Mum? What am I gonna do with me life?" She said, "Yer can't stop me gettin' pregnant when I'm sixteen. I just want a baby."

DIANE

Then all of a sudden I get a boyfriend, then all of a sudden I get a kid, then I have another kid, and then I'm pregnant with another kid. So she said you know, "I would have had everything if you hadn't have met John. Why did you make my dad leave?" I said, "But I never made him leave." But she blamed me 'coz he wasn't here. "If you'd have stayed a single parent he might have come back one day . . ." We had all of this.

PAT

The day she came in and told me she was pregnant . . . we both cried. And I said to her, "No, yer gettin' rid." I said, "It's a baby bringin' up a baby." I said, "I've done it. I've been there. I don't want yer to ruin your life." (*Beat*.) But because she was sixteen I couldn't stop her.

DIANE

She changed from being a loving kind-hearted quiet girl into being an aggressive – well, not aggressive towards anybody else – just me. Because I was the, uh, person that was making her go to school. But I didn't realise the extent of what I was sending her into. I thought it was just girls being a bit . . . And she got all these years of abuse . . . (DIANE *breaks down – trying to compose herself – reassuring the interviewer*.) No it's alright . . . they all used to say to her "trigger, trigger, shoot the nigger" . . . well I didn't know this until she was a heroin addict . . . you know, they did nothing this country to . . . (DIANE *takes some time to compose herself*.) She used to beg me not to go to school, and I used to say, "But you've got to go to school." It was continually arguing . . . One time she even picked up a piece of lego and said I will swallow this if you send me to school. I said well you're going to have to swallow it then because you're going to school. And she did actually swallow a piece of lego. So then I had to phone the doctor's up, didn't I? To find out what it'd do to her. And then she cried and she said, "I'm sorry mum I didn't really mean to swallow it it's just that you're making me go to school." Well I have to live with that every single day. So eventually she come to about fifteen, fifteen and a half when, erm, it come to a head and she said, "I'm running away from home."

(*Lights fade slightly on* PAT *and* DIANE, *although they stay onstage, and pick out* ALI *once more*.)

ACT ONE

Scene Four

ALI I was in a hostel on, erm, London Road, and a lot of the girls that were in there worked the street. I went with a girl just to write, erm, the car registration numbers, she'd been doing it for a while and . . . this girl said, "Come out, Ali, and just take the registration numbers of the cars for me and that would be it." But because I'm a new face out there, we're standing on the corner both withdrawing off the drugs and the fellas gone, "No I don't want you, I want her." I'm a new face, a new face makes money. 'Cos they haven't been there. Something strange to them and that's how it started. And it was terrifying.

(STEPHEN *has come in. He has a mobile phone with him.* ALI *looks at him.*)

You look at someone and y'know if they care or if they don't care, if their eyes are cold . . . you can see it. Windows to the soul.

STEPHEN There are thousands of reasons why people go.

(*He wets a finger tip and cleans a speck of dirt on his shoe.*)

ALI There's no like . . . set face of a punter . . . they all think of a sticky mac and glasses, you know what I mean? It's nothing like that.

STEPHEN Some of them go because . . . well, they want to do things that their wives won't do. Some of them go because it's their opportunity to be with a much younger woman who, under normal circumstances, they could never get into bed with. Others go because they're serial cheaters. Some of them use street girls rather than parlours. I've just never been comfortable with that. It's not something I've ever done.

ALI It depends on the punter. You get the punter . . . he'll sit and talk to you. Half the time he'll say he wants business but he doesn't. He's just . . . a lonely man. And that's it.

(BRIAN *has also come in. He's wearing a shirt that has the name of his business on the breast pocket.*)

BRIAN I was going through a real bad phase. It was like erm, the firm was rocky, my relationship was up the waz, I was in right bad trouble and, eh, this guy was looking for me because I hadn't been able to pay him, in fact, a couple of fellas, and like it was getting really heavy and, em, I got, I was in this mess and I took to picking girls up in the street.

ALI I could say there are evil, dirty, nasty, horrible men. 'Coz there is. But then there's just . . . lonely men . . . needing companionship, nice men.

STEPHEN Some go because they're just absolutely crackers . . . What do I mean? Well . . . I mean, they're bordering on sex offenders. People don't say this but I'll be honest with you – there's a huge – it's a particular hatred of mine. But there is a huge . . . push . . . with a lot of people, parlours, for younger and younger-looking girls . . . girls who may not be underage but, you know, look it . . . they become very very popular, and . . . it's the whole paedophile angle.

ALI I go home I get in the bath and I feel, you know. I, I've scrubbed the ends of my skin raw, sat in bleach and everything – tried to make myself feel cleaner, and it's not (*Makes a short moaning noise.*) . . . it's more what other people put onto you.

BRIAN I stayed out there one day and picked up four girls, or even five. I must've done a hundred quid. In a day! And I was still driving around at ten o'clock at night. And I was like, "What?! Why am I doin' this? I'm up the wall for money, and I just blew a hundred quid." And I mean bloody hell it's a blow-job! Do you know what I mean?

STEPHEN   I mean, people seem to think that, you know, addictions are just something that happens with chemicals you put in your body, and that, but it isn't. There's addictions to gambling, there's addictions to . . . danger . . . there's addictions to . . . bloody physical exercise. If you start getting endorphins pumped in, you start to get the high . . . And there's people who are addicted to sex. (*Little pause.*) I don't think I am.

BRIAN   It blocked, it blocked me mind from the fact that there was a couple of fellas – couple of fellas gonna work me head out.

STEPHEN   I'm not a very addictive personality. I'm a very sort of . . . I'm a fairly balanced person.

BRIAN   I've been doing it for twelve years.

ALI   Prostitution is such a small thing. Prostitution is such a big thing. I can tell you the exact amount of men I have had sex with . . . in all these years. The exact amount of men. Every girl you'll get'll tell ya.

STEPHEN   I've been going to parlours now for about six years. Not to put too fine a point on it, I've got a high sex drive. I got divorced ten years ago . . . my job entailed travelling . . . far east, middle east . . . she got fed up of the fact that every time something went wrong I was four thousand miles away. And what I discovered was . . . after I got divorced was . . . I had a series of . . . bitty and quite argumentative little relationships. Which were totally unfulfilling.

STEPHEN   And I can't go through the rigmarole of one
              night stands. But I kept missing the sex so . . .
              sitting down at the internet, looking through,
              and I happened on a site. Sandy's.

BRIAN   Annie, Suzanne, Debbie – there's loads of them
              I know, loads of them. They're bubbly, they're
              doing what they're doing, they're sound.

STEPHEN   And, in a way, it's perfect. We both know what
              we're there for and that's it.

ALI   It's just a business arrangement. It's not you
              sell yourself for money. No, it's a business
              arrangement.

BRIAN   I've got a lot of time for Debbie. Debbie is
              always boss clean.

ALI   He knows how far he can go, I know how far I
              can go.

BRIAN   I've been for a meal with Debbie, taken her for
              a meal and that. She is, she's spot on, she's a
              diamond. Debbie's on the gear, but she's not
              on the street no more. She works off the phone.
              It's only Debbie I have unprotected with.

ALI   That's it – no emotion, no kissing, no touching
              where I don't want to be touched.

BRIAN   I . . . I . . . I'm dead straight. I treat everybody
              bloody fair.

ALI   Even if they try and kiss your neck it's like
              don't, don't, don't. Your lips . . . awww, come
              near your lips and there's murder. It's made
              clear from the start . . . he gives you the money,
              you do what you've gotta do and that's the
              end of it.

BRIAN   I don't want ye to do it for ten quid, I'll give ye
              twenty five or if I have sex, I'll give ye forty
              quid. I mean don't take the piss out of me and I
              won't take the piss out of you. I mean there's

some girls out there . . . I had six hundred
pound on me. Had it in me side pocket, here.
So, dickhead, jeans are down, she must've
gone in. So I said, listen girl, I got two fellas to
pay. I said, I'm stupid enough to leave it in me
pocket and you took it. She said, don't rape
me. I said, I ain't gonna rape you. Just give me
me dough. I checked through all me pockets,
the floor, under the seats. She hadn't put her
knickers on properly, and I thought it's the
only place it could be and there it was, up her.

ALI   You get the ones that think you're just a piece
           of meat . . . "I can touch your body how I want.
           If it hurts you I don't care."

BRIAN   So, um, I 'got it' – this dough – and I lashed
           her out, down on the docks, just threw her out.
           And I threw her shoes in the water. I said,
           "Fuck you".

ALI   They're just there to be fucked, battered and
           whatever they want off 'em, whatever they
           want to do to them, they can do to 'em. They
           want anal, oral, batter 'em, kick 'em or kill 'em,
           that's what a prostitute is.

BRIAN   I had one girl, she was drunk or drugged, I
           dunno, but when we got to the place where we
           were gonna do the business, I suddenly said to
           meself, nah, I'll sack this girl off. I always tell
           them I've had a line of Charlie and there's
           nothin' down for me. And I see this arl beat up
           Sierra tag on to me. I've clocked these two in
           the mirror. Scag-heads. I had a boss watch on,
           gold chain, couple of hundred quid in me
           pocket. And I thought, she's settin' me up
           here. So. I get to the top of Parley, she said,
           "Pull over here." And I said, "Nah, I'll just turn
           down here" And I spun right round and shot
           the lights and went right down this street . . .
           jumped out the car, "Out!" I went straight to
           Wavertree police station, didn't I? And I said,
           "Listen mate, I've just picked up a girl." He

said, "Yer know yer liable for prosecution?" I
said, "I know I'm liable." I said, "But some poor
sod's gonna come undone with these pair of
bastards. This girl needs sortin'. Somethin'
needs doin' about them." (*Beat.*) He said,
"We'll have a look at it. Go on, bugger off."
And he didn't charge me.

ALI

We're the dirty ones, 'coz we walk the street.
Then there's the sauna girls, that are a little bit
better than us. Then there's what you call
'escorts', yeh? And what d'ya do different,
besides go to a hotel? Liverpool is the Capital
of Culture? Liverpool is the capital of fucking
prostitution! . . . I always remember when I very
first started working . . . Louise Maddison . . .
she's dead now . . . she got killed . . . and, err . . .
Emily Scofield. They sat me in the car – 'coz
I'm only small and slim and – I'm a target
obviously, for big men who think they wanna
bully a woman round, the drunks and all that.
And they sat me down and they said, "Listen,
always be in control." Even if you think you're
not, let them think that you are. "Never go
where he tells ya he's going. You tell him
where you're going. If he won't go there, you
get out the car. Always get your money first
and if you don't feel safe, don't go there."

BRIAN

When I first met her, Nugget, she was in
Adelaide House on a bail charge, 'cause she'd
been done for shopliftin'. All the girls in
Adelaide were on the gear. And they were
doin' the streets. And I was just a customer
when I met her. That was twelve years ago.

ALI

You get the odd punter who'll fall in love with
you. "Oh I'll get you the drugs, I'll keep you in
your drug habit." I've gone through twenty-
seven thousand pounds on a punter. I've made
a punter sell his house.

BRIAN

Oh Christ, well I was sort of, er – I suppose
ye'd call it like in love or lust, but – 'cause

she's tidy like. Ye know she's not a bad lookin' little girl.

ALI   No thee – thee don't fall in love with you thee fall in love with – knight in shining armour. Making them feel good.

BRIAN   I didn't mentally say, "Oh I'll get her off the street and I'll look after her." I just thought she's funny, she was alright, have a laugh with her.

ALI   I say to them: I am gonna pull you down, leave, get out.

BRIAN   She's a heroin user. At one time I used to score for her and cut it into seven days and control it so that the kids could have a mother.

ALI   You will always be a prostitute to him and he will always be a punter. I've seen girls that've married them. Never lasts. Never.

BRIAN   Smack-heads are liars. Everything, everything, from when they open their eyes is just deviousness. It's just, how can I get twenty pound to get a bag of shite. The heartbreak the kids go through. I work all day, I can't relax, I'm worn out – Mrs fucking Doubtfire for Christ's sake, d'ye know what I mean? I tell her this – yer on barley forgets here until these kids are big enough. When they're big enough de ye think I'll be putting up with this crap?

(*He leaves.*)

STEPHEN   I'm not gonna fall in love with the girl and she's certainly not going to fall in love with me. Then, there's the weirdos . . . you know, the . . . I was told about one guy with a foot fetish. Shoes. All he wanted to do was to lick shoes. He'd pay his forty quid, or eighty quid, 'cause he'd stay for an hour, and he'd sit there . . . and, you know, she had to put high heels

on, walk around in them for a couple of minutes
. . . then he would . . . he would just sit there
and lick them. And later, he would try to steal
the shoes. You have no . . . why didn't he just
pay her for the shoes? You tell me.

ALI   No, he takes me to his house right? Gives you
red lipstick to put on, and you've got to smoke
a ciggie, but you've got to pout your lips like
that right? And while you're doing that, he's
got rubber gloves and he's having a wank.
You're not touching him, that's all ye's doing,
smoking a ciggie an' he's got his gas mask.
Right, me nosy arse, I have to know the ins and
outs of everything, and I went to him, "Ay
mate, where the fuck do you get a kink like
that?" And he goes, "When I was seven, I got
took to the dentist, and the receptionist had
bright red lipstick on, red high heels and was
smoking a ciggie. And when I went in and put
the gas mask on I had me first wet dream." And
I went, you will never get it again lad. The first
is the best. After that it doesn't happen. But
that's what he's chasing.

STEPHEN   People come in and steal their knickers as well.
You have no idea what some people do.

ALI   Another fella comes with cakes from Sayers to
throw at him. I said you're wasting these big
cream doughnuts. And I'm slobbering at the
mouth and I've got to throw them at him . . .
Oh, fucking hell. Me mate used to have one . . .
she had a four-poster bed and she used to put
him in a mail bag, you know those Royal Mail
bags? He pinched one. She cut a piece out for
the face part, cut a piece out for his cock . . . tie
him up to the four-poster and leave him there
for ages. She used to go out. She'd come back
. . . wank him for about an hour . . . then leave
him . . . then wank him again . . . when he was
on the verge of coming she used to stop. She
got three hundred quid for that! . . . Big mad
kinks.

STEPHEN   I mean, you get the other ones . . . I know it
          goes on but it's a total closed book to me. Pain.
          Oh Jesus, no. I can't see that one at all.

ALI   It's like, erm, naughty and nice, and – you
          know them typa things? Ye know when you've
          got a bruise and you touch it but it hurts. 'Ave
          yer ever done it and you keep touching it and
          you know it's going to hurt when you touch it
          but you touch. Like and I go to him, is that
          what it's like? Like touching it, and you know
          it's gonna hurt but you go ooh . . .

STEPHEN   You get these blokes, and they'll walk in and
          . . . there's a heavy piece of wood there . . .
          imagine a cricket bat . . . and he gets them to
          get two hands on it . . . and, I mean, he stands
          there, and, you know, and she tells me she's
          working up a sweat, she says it's hard work.
          And this guy's getting off on it. Yeah! On his
          arse. And the other side, thank you very much.

ALI   Is that what it is, that little, 'Ooh, ooh,'? Ye
          know or when you're trying to go to the toilet
          and then, 'Ahhh.' Is that it? Do ye know? Ye
          just can't fathom them. Then you get the nappy
          men. Men who wanted to be treated like kids, in
          nappies, stay with the bottle. And the button
          man. He used to bring a shiny red button. You
          know the foreskin? He used to want you to sew
          the red button in there, he brought the needle
          and cotton with him. Now you tell me who's the
          most damaged?

          (*Lights fade on* ALI *and* STEPHEN.)

          Scene Five

          The Mothers

PAT   I've never known anyone go through a
          pregnancy like that in me life. It was awe

inspirin'. Because she never moaned the whole time she was pregnant. She woke me up the day she was in labour and I didn't believe her.

They gave her pethadine, she was as high as a kite. The only thing Pauline said was, "This is Mickey Mouse's fault." As she gave birth. "This is Mickey Mouse's fault." 'Cause she was high . . . on the Pethadine.

DIANE   I brought social services involved because I thought they might talk to her. They sent out – what do you call them when the couples split up? – a, a mediator. But it didn't work because she was doing religion. Hanane kept saying, "Don't preach to me mother, she doesn't believe in God." (DIANE *laughs*.) So they put us in touch with Tim. Working for Barnardos. And, er, he overstepped his mark well and truly. He used to say to me, "Well, she could do with a break away from you. Obviously it's doing the pair of you no good arguing and bickering in front of the other children." So he took her to a place in Norfolk. She could come in as long as it was before eleven o'clock at night, she could smoke, she didn't have to go to school. She's fifteen!

PAT   Anyway. She had the baby. James. And she wanted to bring this baby up on her own. She kept saying to me, "I'm not saying he's the father mum because he raped me." I said, "How could he rape you when you were going out with him, Pauline?" She said, "I didn't say yeah." And right till six months before she died, she said she wanted nothing more to do with this man. Anyway, she gets to seventeen. She comes strollin' in one day . . . "I met this fella Mum. He's brilliant. He's a taxi driver. He loves the baby. And he's gonna look after me." We had a row. Because I didn't like him. This Billy Dalesworth. Anyway, next thing, she packed up and she went. Took the baby with

her. And I never seen her, er, for nearly twelve
months.

(*She lights up a cigarette.*)

DIANE   So then she moved to this hostel in Holywell
when she was just before sixteen. She met this
nice lad, as I thought. Well he was a nice lad. It
wasn't his fault he was in the hostel. He'd been
shifted from foster home to foster home.
Anyway Zenon – was the boyfriend's name –
he'd been a heroin addict.

PAT   One day I gets a phone call from her. She just
said, "Mum, I wanna come home." She didn't
tell me nothin'. So I, yer know, that's me
daughter, I'm gonna come and get yer. I
brought her and the baby home. He'd locked
her in a room, this Billy. Wouldn't let her out of
the house. If she didn't do as she was told
she'd get a hiding. (*Beat.*) And, erm, I still
didn't know nothin' about the drugs. Really
didn't. This is how stupid I am. I thought she
was just tired all the time.

DIANE   She was struggling with who she was . . . She
had a problem with . . . she was a very, uhm . . .
like that personality, you know . . . Once she
got hold of something made her feel better 'coz
she didn't like the person she was, she would
take anything to make her feel . . . to . . . you
know, to get away from people calling her Paki
or whatever. So then it got worse then, didn't
it? 'Coz they were calling her a smack-head
now as well.

(*Lights fade on* PAT *and* DIANE.)

Scene Six

CATHERINE *is in her fifties, dressed in dark, loose cloth
trousers and a big black cardigan. Her manner is worn-out*

but completely alert. She shuffles around a kitchen area in her
stocking feet. Shouting through to the interviewer.

CATHERINE   I have a sister who is severely mentally ill. You
                  could say I am as well . . . (*Laughs.*) but she is
                  severely mentally ill and I had not been
                  satisfied with the level of resources. And I was
                  teaching in Halewood, decent, hard working
                  families; no reason why they couldn't get a
                  job, except that the city had just had jobs
                  sucked out of it. This was around 1981. They
                  were I guess the two major reasons I got into
                  politics.

                  (*The* INSPECTOR *enters, carrying a mug of*
                  coffee, his helmet under his arm. He's a
                  healthy, fit-looking man in his mid-40s. He's
                  wearing a protective body vest. He's in the
                  middle of telling an anecdote. He's enjoying
                  the telling of it.)

KEVIN   I ride . . . this sounds terribly corny, but I ride
                  my bike to work and I get excited . . . I do . . .
                  getting towards the station . . . because . . .
                  "Oh, what's going to happen today?" and . . .
                  it's genuine, that. (*Sound of laughter from*
                  outside, a couple of people.) Most days, I'll be
                  out there on my bike even if it's just for half an
                  hour, an hour, so the people who live here see
                  me as visibly doing what a policeman should
                  do – despite the fact that I'm an inspector . . .
                  not today . . . 'cause I got ratted last night and
                  I just didn't feel like it, so um . . . actually we
                  all went out last night . . . Yeah, if we've got a
                  campaign running, which I'm just about to start
                  on prostitution – reducing it, breaking the
                  cycle, all the usual stuff, we don't –

                  (*The laughter increases, more people joining*
                  in.)

KEVIN   There was a bit of a fight last night . . . which
                  some of the officers were involved in . . . and
                  there was a poster . . . about drinking too much

and some speech bubbles have been put on it.
(*He laughs.*) Very humorous. In this job there
is a lot of banter and I don't think it'll ever be
stopped. Where were we? . . . Yeah. The job.
It's very stressful. It is. But it's good stress.
(*Beat. With a smile.*) I'm twenty years service
today.

CATHERINE   Just over two years ago we began to have quite
a lot of, er, concern expressed by local
residents about prostitution on their doorstep.
Local communities were beginning to feel very
badly threatened. And I guess by the May or
June it became quite obvious that the police
were not in a position to be able to do anything
about this.

KEVIN   Whenever we run a police operation, there's
always displacement issues. Police are very
good at it, we'll move it, we'll sort it for you in
two minutes flat but it doesn't get rid of it.
Walton Lane, we do a campaign, push it over
town, town'll do one, push it into Everton. It
just keeps getting spread and spread and
spread.

ALI   We get pushed further and further out, the
police come round and they're having a purge
– So everybody starts going out, out, into
where there's no houses you can run to, no
shops and they're dead isolated.

CATHERINE   When the motion first went to the council, it
went out as a motion for brothels, which I just
don't think work. That was, I think in the June
or July, 2003, and the murder was shortly
beforehand: two prostitutes whose bodies were
found dismembered in bin bags. Which sort of
brought everything into focus. A colleague of
mine said that she thought managed zones
ought to be brought in, rather than tolerance
zones, and she said, "Will you write the
amendment for me?" (*Laughs slightly.*) I
thought, "Well hang on a minute."

Oh God, I'm not devout. Dear God, no I'm not devout. I have not been what you would call a devout Catholic, but the beliefs are still there, and I don't think that when you believe that something is right, that you can just hide it. And I think that prostitution is wrong.

But – I wrote the amendment. Erm, and when it came to council, I voted against it: but the majority didn't, so we ended up with something that I had not believed in . . . and as the executive member, it was my responsibility to make sure it was carried out . . .

KEVIN

Erm, we've got a new chief and I agree hands down – I'm not being political here, I do agree with what he says – a managed zone won't break the cycle. It's not really putting the support in for the prostitutes.

CATHERINE

I'll tell you exactly what's gonna happen. The zone would have, probably a hundred to a hundred and fifty yards of main road as its frontage. There would be CCTV, lighting, there would be a uniformed presence on site. There will be services for the girls, counselling services, medical services, which would say to them, look you know, if you really want to get out of this, this is what we can do for you, and we can do this tomorrow, not in six weeks, not ten weeks, we can do it tomorrow.

ALI

I think . . . as long as . . . it's like all confidential, y'know, they're not going to get letters sent in to their wives, all things like that – 'coz then it makes them angry when they've been arrested and then it leads to girls getting beat up and things 'coz they blame the girl obviously.

CATHERINE

Where you stop there's a breezeblock wall. You can't open the driver's door. On the women's side you can because there's a footpath, so

Safety
&
resources

ALI

they can get out if they need to. When they've
finished their business whatever, they have to
sort of reverse there to go round.

And . . . I don't mean stick them in the middle
of a residential area, I mean, well if it's gonna
be a managed zone, have someone in a box, like
a typa' security – he does manage the zone.

CATHERINE

It would be set aside for this purpose at night,
say from eight in the evening, until three or
four the following morning. So there would be
no tolerance to street based prostitution during
the day, at all, or anywhere else in the city.
Okay?

KEVIN

They're still going to be prostituting
themselves for drugs. Generally that's why
they're selling themselves.

CATHERINE

This is actually a police issue, it's not a local
council issue. I think the question needs to be
asked of them: "What are you doing?"

KEVIN

Drugs is, without a shadow of a doubt, behind
the current problems with prostitution . . . and
breaking the cycle is difficult because it's not a
police, it's not a traditional police . . . direction
. . . we've always been enforcement . . . and
we're just, we're getting quite pink and fluffy
now, for want of a better expression . . . and
people don't see it as right that we're not
enforcing.

ALI

Every girl out there wants safety 'cos at the
moment every girl is terrified. Someone will be
in the street with marks all over them, d'you
know, and you go, "What happened to you?"
"Oh some punter last night, blah, blah . . ."

KEVIN

If you have a safe zone, say down by the
warehouses, by the docks, where no one lives,
it's very non-residential, you're probably
making the sex workers even more vulnerable.

CATHERINE   You say that what we're . . . suggesting, is the
             wrong way to do it? Then tell us the right way
             to do it. Show us what you're going to do,
             show us on the streets what you're going to
             do. You're saying that you're gonna put police
             officers on the street but actually not doing it.

KEVIN   My targets – they're on the wall here – split
             into sub groups: violence, robbery, burglary,
             theft – prostitution's not on there. And that
             makes you direct your resources accordingly,
             because if I'm not being judged on how many
             prostitutes I'm arresting, or how many kerb
             crawlers I'm arresting, why bother?

CATHERINE   Well, the situation is, we've done everything
             that we can as a council. All the reports and
             the formal requests to set up a managed area
             have all gone to the home office now. (*She
             places a bulky folder on the table.*) The
             biggest obstacle, really, if it happens, will be
             that politicians in government will lose their
             nerve. Whether they will give it the go ahead
             or not, I really don't know. It will mean a
             change in the law. (*She leaves.*)

ALI   Me honest opinion? It depends on how they're
             managed.

BRIAN   I've heard the girls talking about it, and they
             say, "Nah, wouldn't work." And I wouldn't be
             going there. Thee'd be taking yer registration
             number and videoing and I wouldn't want – I
             personally wouldn't go there. (*He leaves.*)

KEVIN   I would develop what the Armistead are doing.
             The knowledge is there, the passion is there.
             With the correct sort of funding they could
             develop a full support network. But it would
             take a lot of money. (*Looking at* ALI, *who
             remains.*) I've met quite a few of the
             prostitutes . . . you chat to them when you're
             waiting for the van to turn up . . . We just go

and talk to them and that's what a lot of police activity is. Just going up and having a chat.

ALI   There's three police officers – when I got kidnapped, right? He was at my bedside every single night, teddybears, everything, Peter Curry, and now he's been moved up to the flying squad, you know for serious crimes, what's the other one's name? I can't remember. He's erm, oh God he was lovely, his sister's a heroin addict, absolutely brilliant man.

KEVIN   You feel sorry for them. It's not just about locking them up and . . . we don't get them in the back of the van and give them a hiding or whatever. We actually care about these girls. We really do, but if – if someone's gotta be dealt with, we'll deal with them and we'll deal with them really, really firmly if we have to.

ALI   There's this Derek – this is a sergant in St Anthony's, pulls up in a van, "Get in Cows. I'm herding up the cows. Get in."

KEVIN   I mean, it's happened, of course it's happened, it's always going to happen 'cause there's rogue police officers.

ALI   The total lack of respect off police officers where . . . (*Addresses* KEVIN *directly.*) "Listen, he's just raped me" . . . "You're a prostitute, how could he rape you" . . . "It was a business arrangement. I said no. No means no." Whatever context you take it in, no means no. Listen. I said no. I said no. I mean we've got the reg of the car, the description, the man, all of it. He's up there, you're there. (*Gestures imbalance with her hands.*) No. No. Until we're on an equal par . . . (*She turns away in disgust.*)

KEVIN   There was another prostitute that was killed . . . in Kensington . . . I don't really want to give you her name for confidentiality reasons . . .

but again, a very sad case really . . . chaotic
lifestyle, poly-drug user, barking mad. And a
week before she was killed I'd arrested her. I
was sat up on the hill . . . near the park . . . on
my mountain bike, in my uniform, eating my
sandwiches. She gave me a Joey. A false name.
So basically, from speaking to her . . . she gave
me her correct details . . . and she was in
breach of her previous anti-social behaviour
order. So she was arrested . . . and I think she
. . . she was probably out on bail for that when
she was killed.

(*Little pause.* KEVIN *is on his own now.*)

I've found . . . there's situations throughout
my career that you cry . . . you've gotta,
you've gotta go . . . I mean, people react
differently of course, but, you go into, you've
gotta go into a room on your own sometimes,
some of the things you see . . . you've gotta go
into a room on your own . . .

(*Picks up a photo.*)

That's my daughter. She's fifteen now. I took
her through the district recently . . . you know,
to show her what happens if you start using
drugs . . . it's quite frightening I think. (*Little
pause.*) I don't know what she'll be. She's a
girl. One minute it's a teacher, the next it's a
doctor. (*Little pause.*) She's learning to fly . . .
at school . . . with the Combined Cadet Force.

Scene Seven

The Mothers

DIANE   I'd take her down the co-op and I'd buy her
bags of potatoes and milk and even cigarettes
. . . So she used to go back to Holywell on the
bus with bags and bags of shopping, and she
used to be laughing. I'd put her on the bus and

then, all the way home me mouth would be
going . . . like this . . . I'd come in the house
and I'd say, "Got to go toilet, got a bad
stomach . . ." I'd go in the bathroom, and I'd
break me heart. And the kids'd be in here,
watching telly. They wouldn't even know that I
was absolutely breaking me heart, 'coz I was
putting her on a bus basically to go to a hostel
and that, as a mother, you don't do.

PAT   I was workin' in the snooker hall at the time,
and this fella used to come in. His name was
Mickey. Big man. Big huge man. He was in the
army. And he took a fancy to Pauline. And
Pauline bein' Pauline, thinkin' that, yer know . . .
'this man's gonna look after me . . .' (*Little
pause.*) Next thing, she gets a place down in
Bark Road. She said, "Yer must come down
Mum, any time yer want." And I didn't bother.
I never really bothered until she'd been there
about twelve months. I went down to see her . . .
and this Mickey was sittin' there. (*Beat.*) But
the change in him. I couldn't believe it. I went,
"What the hell happened to you?" "I've got . . .
got a bad back. Been on medication." So I
never said nothin'. This is how stupid I am.
Didn't know nothin'. (*Little pause.*) And
Pauline came here one day . . . to visit . . . and
me mate was here, Yvonne, and she took one
look at our Pauline and she said, "And how
long have yer been on heroin?" (*Little pause.*)
Well, yer could've knocked me down with a
feather. I went, "What?" Yvonne . . . she knew
straight away. Because of her family. She said,
"Pauline, tell yer mother the truth. I know when
somebody's an addict. Because I've lived with
it for over twenty years." (*Pause.*) Pauline
broke down. And I broke down. Next thing and
we're cuddling each other. "Please Mum, help
me, help me." I said, "I'll get yer through this.
We'll work it out together, yer know? It's not a
problem. We'll get it sorted."

ALI   Me mum says, "What did I do wrong?" My
             mum didn't do nothing wrong. I had the most
             beautiful parents anyone would ask for. I was
             brought up proper . . . I just got (*Pause.*) . . .
             the wrong people, the wrong time in me life . . .
             know what I mean?

PAT   Brought her back home. And I never left her.
             For four days I stayed with her. She was
             hallucinatin' . . . about the baby . . . seein' the
             baby lyin' dead. Four days we sat and she
             stank. I had to lift her up and put her in the
             bath . . . washed, cleaned, back in her pyjamas,
             back on the couch. And I thought great, she's
             doin' really well. This is gonna work. (*Little
             pause.*) Then this Mickey came down. He said
             . . . "Okay Pat, I'll stay with her. You go to
             work." So I said, "Alright Mick, thanks," yer
             know, 'cause I needed the money. And when I
             come in she was all happy and . . . well . . . I
             didn't know . . . (*She takes a sip of water.*) . . .
             He'd come down with a bag of smack to give to
             her. He was usin' her. Because Pauline was his
             money. (*Little pause.*) Pauline was his money.

ALI   Man I met was a drug dealer. He came out of
             prison and he had no money to sell drugs and
             all that. The first time I ever . . . he brought two
             Pakistani blokes back and that's how it all
             started. I didn't know I'd ever smoked heroin. I
             thought I was smoking pot oil. It's the devil's
             dust. Makes you do anything.

PAT   I think Pauline had told him what Billy
             Dalesworth had done, and he's thought, "Hang
             on, I could do that." So this is what he done.
             He was usin' her. Like Billy Dalesworth did.
             But I didn't know this at the time.

DIANE   They send all the heroin addicts to this doctor
             because he's the only one in Holywell that can
             deal out Me – erm, what de you call it? –
             Methadone. One day I said to Lee, which is the
             drugs councillor – Lee was absolutely brilliant

– he comes from Liverpool – he knows everything he needs to know.

(LEE *has come in and is listening to what* DIANE *is saying.*)

I said, "Er, I'm going to phone the doctor up and make sure she's taking Thyroxin." Because she had an under active thyroid.

LEE   Don't phone him.

DIANE   Why?

LEE   No, don't phone him at all. Hanane is coming down to tell you why.

DIANE   So she arrived and I said, "Well – why don't, why doesn't everybody want me to phone this doctor?" "'Cause he abused me." He asked her to do rude things to him so he'd give her methadone. He told her to go to Rhyl. He said, "I use the brothel in Rhyl. Why don't you go and earn yourself some decent money?" She never visited another doctor from leaving Holywell to being found dead.

LEE   I'd heard rumours before about this doctor.

DIANE   He put her on that road without a doubt. What he did to her.

LEE   As far as I'm concerned, the doctor never put her onto that life, it had started. The first time I met Hanane I was covering the Wrexham area. This young slip of a thing – beautiful young girl – sat down crying. She was under Jenny at the time and Jenny kept telling me, "Oh Hanane's doing really well, she just has a little use now and again", and I just went (*Whispered.*) Bollocks.

I'd said to Hanane, "I believe you're going over to Liverpool. Where you going?" She

said, "I'm going to, er, to Bootle."
"Whereabouts?", and she said, "People's
houses and all that." And I was like (*Makes
sucking noise.*) "I don't really think darling
. . ." – I think she was about fifteen at the time
– I said, "I don't really think you're cut out for
that." She just had a fascination for scousers
and Liverpool. I said to Jenny there are people
out there in Liverpool, wanna take advantage
of her they will do. I said, "Let's face it, she's a
gorgeous looking kid." And so it was quite
frightening. I just sat her down and said,
"Look". I said, "Let's, let's put the bullshit
away. I think you're being exploited Hanane,
by various people. I know that your mother
does love you. You don't think that she does,
but she does, and I know that you can be a
stubborn little cow. Ye mam is not going to
immediately take you back. Yer mam's gonna
want to see you clean."

DIANE   Lee said to me, "I don't need to see you.
You're a parent, and I know you mean well by
it, but she's got to come to me, beg me she can
come off drugs, because it's only her word I'll
take for it."

And her life changed so much. This is where
she come off the drugs completely. She went
after him and she begged him to take her off
the drugs, and he did . . . she was off for quite
a while actually. Months. And then, I'm
walking down the street and I'd never seen Lee
in me life before, and I'm walking down the
street, and she goes "Hiya Mum!" And I went
. . . (*A look of amazement.*) 'coz she had her
hair down here and it was, you know, I hadn't
seen Hanane for a long time with her hair loose
on the street. And I went, oh bloody hell! Hah!
I was so shocked. Anyway, Lee said . . .

LEE   She looks amazing, doesn't she?

DIANE   I said, "Bloody hell she does!" Lee is the only
         one that got her to wear her hair down and got
         her confidence back like you've never seen.
         Like when she was so high, she used to be so
         bubbly and I'd go shopping with her, and she
         made me and the kids spaghetti Bolognese and
         she made us tea and she was back to her
         normal self. She had all her confidence. She
         was absolutely glowing. She was lovely. Just
         how we were when she was little and then . . .
         then he come back out of prison, and I can't
         blame him because he loved her.

LEE   I can't remember his name. Zenon. That's it.
         'Krypton.' The inert gas. (*He leaves.*)

DIANE   They were just trying to keep her away from
         him, and Hanane didn't want that. She ran away
         with him to Birmingham, and he went with this
         other girl. When she came back, she said, "The
         cheating bastard has cheated on me." So I
         thought, well is this good or is this bad? 'Coz
         without him she . . . she could get off the drugs
         again. I know it's not his fault because his
         sister burnt herself to death. They turned off
         her life support machine when she was eleven,
         in front of his face. So I did actually feel sorry
         for him, but . . . Zenon wasn't really good for
         her. But he did love her. And you want to see
         the poem – I'll show you the poem he wrote
         about her 'cause he really did feel guilty.
         (*Pause.*) They wouldn't let him out of prison to
         go to her funeral.

PAT   Anyway they moved from here, 'cause I
         thought she was clean. The next thing was . . .
         this man knocked on me door. And, but the
         man's dead now, God bless him but, he
         knocked on me door, with this, like, folder. He
         asked me if I was Pauline's Mum, and I went,
         "Yeah, why?" He said, "Look . . . " He said,
         "She really needs your help." So I said, "Well,
         who are you." He said, "I'm just a very good
         friend of hers." So I brought him in. He said,

"We've been to the top of your road on a number of occasions, but she's too frightened." He said, "She's alright at the minute but . . . I'm really worried about her. She wants to come home. But she's with this fella whose not gonna let her go because she's earnin' money for him." So I asked him what he meant and . . . oh, God . . . when he told me . . . (*She starts to cry.* BILLY *takes a tissue from a box and brings it to her. He returns to sofa/chair, and his newspaper.* PAT *needs a little time to compose herself.*) When he told me what she was doin' . . . I wrecked this house. I wrecked it.

ALI   How me mum found out was . . . I was arrested and kept in custody for not turning up in court. They kept me in all weekend. The sergeant who was on, drank in me sister's pub. He told me mum. She's very Catholic. She was in court on the Monday with me sister. "There's your spare keys to your flat, I don't want to see you again." I didn't speak to her for three and a half years.

DIANE   Hanane phoned me from Liverpool police station. She goes, "Hi mum, it's me." And I goes, "Oh where are you?" And she said, "Liverpool." She says, "I lived on the streets in Rhyl practically. No harm come to me there. What harm can come to me in Liverpool?" Anyway, she said, "I can't stay on the phone. I'm calling you from a police station. I've been arrested." "Oh for God's sake," I said, "What have you pinched this time?" "Nothing. I'm working the streets." "Well," she said, "I've got to go now," and she was in tears, so she put the phone down and, uhm, I cried . . . sat up and cried all night.

PAT   I got the biggest man out of the Eden Vale that I know. And when we got there . . . they were in this hovel on the dock road. It was stinkin'. The baby was filthy. Pauline was lyin' in a bed of filth. And there was no sign of Mickey. He'd put nails through all the windows, er, and padlocked the bedroom door so she couldn't get out. She was trapped. And I just took – (*Takes another tissue.*) Thanks love. I just took one look at her. I said, "Get yer gear on and get out.' I said, "Yer comin' home with me." I grabbed the baby, left everythin' there . . . and I brought her home. And we did the same thing again. Everything we could . . . to get her off the stuff.

ALI   You find the shimmer falls off, yeh, there's fuck-all glamorous about it, do you know what I mean? Going to clubs when I was fifteen, getting in just 'cos he had a few bob, drinking champagne at fifteen, snorting Charlie, do you know what I mean? I thought I was the bees knees.

DIANE   Hanane believed anything. If you said to her there was a pot of gold at the bottom of the river she'd dive in just to see it. She'd believe anything anybody ever told her. And that was the trouble, the half of it, she was too naïve.

PAT   She must have been about twenty-one. Going to her mates every day. Me looking after the baby. She didn't go out in the afternoon, she went out at night. It didn't bother me, because she's a young girl. (*Pause.*) And then she turned round and said to me she'd met this fella. Rob Fairwell. He worked for a solicitor. He had a Jeep. And he had his own house in Southport. And first time I met him, he walked in with half a bottle of, er, brandy. Bottle of coke. And a box of chocolates. And I thought, "Oh, I like him." (*She laughs.*) The first time any fella's ever done this, I really like this one. Good job, got his own house. Brilliant. He took her away for three days, took her pot-holin'. Loved it. On my life, she loved it. And I thought, "Oh he's great, him. A lovely man." Maybe this time . . . maybe it's all gonna be fine.

ALI   My baby become me addiction. I got clean. Nothing. I lived for that baby and I knew every day, I used to wanna wake him up before he woke up and . . . mad stupid things, when I think back now. Was even jealous when people were holding him.

PAT   And Pauline, she said to me, "What am I goin' to tell him mum?" So I said, "Well, tell him the truth." She said, "I can't. He'll leave me." I said, "Yer've gotta sit down . . . and yer've gotta tell the man. Because he won't be able to help yer, until he knows what's goin' on." So she went upstairs, sat him down, and told him. (*Beat*.) I was downstairs with the baby. And she come down . . . about an hour later . . . cryin' . . . and she said, "He says it's gonna be okay. He's gonna take me away . . . out where there's no way I can get any stuff . . . and we're gonna get clean." Brilliant. That's all I want. Is for her to get clean. And I thought, I've got no qualms with this man. I had no worries about him at all. I thought, this is really gonna work. This is good. (*She smiles*.)

ALI   We'd been to a birthday party the night before and, er, he was like an alarm clock . . . used to wake up half past seven every morning but I . . . I . . . I . . . he was in a routine but we'd been late coming in from this birthday party, so at quarter to eight, the baby – he's slept in, you know, and I went back to sleep – biggest mistake of me life.

But he'd . . . he'd been dead for hours. There was asbestos in the mattress. Erm, you know the way they take the cot – oh, you get questioned and everything – suspicious circumstances and everything. As soon as I opened the room I knew he was dead. It took seven hours for them to get him out my arms though.

It was just, "He's okay, he's gonna wake up in a minute". They were like, "Alright, can we just take him the hospital Ali, to check him over?" I said, "Well let me get his bottles ready, and his nappies and his clothes." I was convinced he was waking up. Once I knew . . . I let him . . . that was it. And it took a long . . . a long time, but . . . I will give them that. They were brilliant, they were brilliant. I just walked. Put me in a body bag. If I can stand up after that mate . . . give me anything now. Then I was back on the gear.

(Lights fade. End of Act One.)

ACT TWO

Scene One

The Drop In – Part Two

ANDY *and* COLIN *in the background 'setting up' thermoses, etc, that we saw at the start of the play. We hear the noise of a buzzer and* MARCIA *comes bursting through the doors at the back.*

MARCIA   Fuckin' hell. It's freezin' out there! Is that hot choccie?

COLIN   Soup. Tomato. Want some?

MARCIA   Fucking soup? Go head then. Get on this. Or, hey. Look at the chocolates and the candles an all that. Looks lovely, doesn't it? (*Helping herself to the soup, referring to chocolates.*) Get us some of the purple ones, they're me favourites. (*About the soup.*) Who made this? Not enough salt. Minge-bag.

COLIN   Hey. I slaved all day over that, Mrs.

MARCIA   Where? In Tescos? Only messing. It's tasty, nice.

ALI   (*coming on, rubbing her arm with her sleeve rolled up*) Me war wounds, me war wounds, look! That friggin' doctor! (*Sees* MARCIA, *goes to hug her – warm, affectionate, excited to see her.*) Hiya baby! You alright queen? (*They embrace.*)

MARCIA   Hiya, yer alright? (*Gesturing to candles.*) When did she get buried?

ALI   Yesterday.

MARCIA   Did ye go?

ALI   Yeh I did.

ANDY   (*noticing* MARCIA, *comes over*) Twice in one
             week? We are honoured. Don't need to ask
             your date of birth, do we? (MARCIA *laughs,
             goes back to talking to* ALI. *Filling in the
             form, to himself.*) Where did I put that other
             box of condoms?

MARCIA   Have you done the Belgians yet? Down at the
             docks?

ALI   Is there a ship in?

MARCIA   Wear trackies though, 'cause you have to climb
             over this big thing to get on board.

             (COLIN *notices* ANDY *is still searching for the
             box of condoms.*)

COLIN   Under there. Who's still waiting to see the
             doctor?

ALI   There's a few nice pairs of kecks here. (*Holds
             up a pair – sequinned – for her to inspect.*)

             (COLIN *gets up, goes to look at the list.*)

MARCIA   If they were black I'd have them ones.
             (*Looking through the makeup, trying on two
             brands on the back of her hand.*) Don't want
             to look like a clown. It's too white, that one.

ANDY   (*interacting with the girls looking through
             clothes*) There's still someone in with her.

ALI   (*holding up an ugly pair of jeans, big, baggy,
             decorated with some appliquéd badges*) If we
             wear these people'll know us as drug users.

MARCIA   Got any of those rape alarms?

ANDY   In the box on the table there.

MARCIA	Can you get pulled if you're carrying a blade and it's under a certain size?

COLIN	No. You can't carry a blade. It's an offensive weapon, you'd be arrested right away if they catch you with that on you.

ALI	Arrested? You know they say there was five hundred prositutes working in Liverpool at the arrest count, it's 'coz they're arresting the same ones fifteen times a night. They nick you every time they see you. About six times in one night. . . .

(DENNI *has come in and catches the end of this. Loud, big personality.*)

DENNI	Fucking five hundred prostitutes me arse. (*To* ALI.) Hiya baby! When did you get out? (*They embrace.*) Hey, have ye heard, Jane's got out as well! She's up in Brighton – on the Subutex!

ALI	The miracle drug? Ye fucking joking. We cut it with something else in the nick, it was like having five bags of rock. I was like that, doing me cell! (*Makes scrubbing motions.* DENNI *bursts out laughing, turns into the throes of a coughing fit. She sits down on the floor.* ALI *looks at* DENNI.) You alright? (*Goes over to her, wipes the sweat off her brow with her hand.*)

DENNI	Crack chest. I know . . . I'm sweatin. Just getting over pneumonia. Girl throw us a bag of them over there. I can't get up 'cause of me leg.

ANDY	(*comes over*) How're you doing? Leg still bad?

DENNI	Leg bad? I can't ride me bike. (*Laughter.*) The fella's up in court this week. He blagged me to get out the car, shut the door, I put me hand in the window, he's only wound the window up, started the car, right? A police man found me right – me skirt had been ripped off, ye know

off all the bushes and the branches, where he
drove me in to the wall, I've just been found
with a pair of boots and a top on, and that was
it. Me leg. I ended up – (*To* Ali, *who is putting
lots of clothes into a bin bag.*) Ah, save me
some clothes! (*Back to her story.*) I had
abrasions from me head to me toe right down.
There. Feel them. I've got, erm, two big holes
here. They took a big square piece of skin there
and one on the other leg, 'cause I was left with
two big holes, and a shattered knee cap.

Andy   He's gonna go to court.

Denni   No he's been done. He got bottom section
            eighteen.

Andy   What does that mean?

Denni   Er, it's the next one down from attempted
            murder. So what they've done, erm, he's he's
            admitted it and like he's gone to court now we
            haven't got to 'ave to a erm, what is –
            what is it when ye got to court and yer 'ave like
            a –

Andy   Solicitor?

Denni   No, no. What is it called? Where yer 'ave yer
            have te – I have te go to court and when they
            admit it. Yer 'ave a, erm. Colin, what de ye call
            it, that? Ali what de ye call it when ye go to
            court?

Ali   (*from a distance, helping herself to soup*) A
            trial.

Denni   A trial. Because he went guilty I didn't have to
            go to a trial.

Marcia   Am I okay to take these little bits?

Colin   Yes you are darling.

MARCIA	Thanks. God bless. (*She leaves.*)
JILL	(*running in, also rough, loud and high*) Bottle of Jack. Bottle of Jack! I come here last week, and this, this, this . . . (*Referring to* ALI.) . . . always gets first pick! She's walking round thinking she was the chick of the nib on the beat.
ALI	First come first served.
JILL	Ooh, hark at Goldilocks there!
ANDY	(*to* JILL) Decided to pay us a visit have you?
JILL	Yeh! I'm gonna smoke me dolly and get meself injected. (*Rooting through clothes.*) I want that one there.
COLIN	Oh she put those aside, they're for her.
JILL	Shut up and mind your own business. (*Clocking a bag on the front row.*) Whose is that?
ANDY	(*referring to the audience*) Hers.
JILL	'Cos I'd have had that . . . (*Laughs.*) No I wouldn't. I'm not like that. Am I like that?
ANDY	Depends what day it is, love.
JILL	(*unfolding what looks like pair of leather trousers*) Oh my God they're hotpants. (*Carries on shuffling through clothes, addressing* DENNI – *she's the natural boss.*) Put all these back here. Somewhere I can wash me feet before I put that on?
COLIN	Yeh, just round there.
JILL	Chuck us a chocolate. Don't be leaving all the shite ones. (ALI *throws her a chocolate. Chewing on chocolate, looking at* DENNI *holding a top and skirt up, addresses*

ACT TWO

audience.) Imagine that top, that skirt with them. You'd get twenty fuckin' years wouldn't you? You'd get a ten stretch in' the fuckin' dingle, wouldn't you? Talk about three strikes and yer out? They'd give you fuckin' ten.

ANDY   (*indicating audience*) Ye going to talk to these?

JILL   Before I've had me fuckin' drink? Go 'ead. Alright then.

(*She comes forward.*)

How long have I been doing this? 'Bout twenty odd years. I come out of care and that. Gear, innit? I was like sixteen, she was twenty-one. Got me habit sky-high, got me on rock. Every time I see her she gets a slap. I smash her face in every time I see her. First time? Oh fuckin' terrifying, yeh. 'Course it was. I shit meself. Didn't rob them then or nothing. Now? Fuckin' rinse them. Yeah rinse them. Anyone, anything. Then, I'm just like terrified getting ten quid. Now, I'll just see what they've got. And if they come back and see me later, they fuckin' have to deal with me, I'll fuckin' knock them out. (*Pause.*) When I see sixteen year-olds now? I swerve them. It's fuckin' sick, it's noncin', isn't it? I don't even speak to them. They knock me sick. And if I seen a fella with them I'd punch their fuckin' head in. It's noncin'. (*She has finished with us. Exiting to loos.*) Denni, you going straight out from here?

(*She exits.*)

DENNI   Too right I'm rattlin'. (*To worker, eating soup.*) Ye know what? Ye know next time use a bit more salt in it.

COLIN   (*sarcastic*) Oh I'm sorry. I'm sorry.

ANDY   Denni, have you got somewhere to crash tonight?

DENNI   I need a lie-in, me.

ANDY   Alright, so ye've got somewhere.

DENNI   I'm waiting to go in to the Kevin White. I had a bed on the Wednesday but, but I had me health issues to attend to because of all the crap that went on and shit, so I dunno.

ANDY   When you came in that night in the Armistead, and I went out for a fag with you.

DENNI   I was, I was a wreck, weren't I? I'm having counselling and the lot, ye know? It's just done me head in totally. One of the working girls said, "Did ye go to the funeral?" And I said, "Nobody told me." I thought Sheila woulda told me of all people.

ALI   I found out off Lucy.

(JILL *has just come back after being injected.*)

JILL   Oh that was fuckin' 'arl arse. No one told us about it. I got told last night. (JILL *continues to rant loudly in the background about not having been told about the funeral, and the outreach workers attempt to comfort her, but only certain sections are clear.*) No I'm not saying – just no one told me . . . No one told me about the funeral . . . It's just fuckin' 'arl arse, de ye know what I mean?

DENNI   (*overriding* JILL) Well there ye go then, I got told last night. No one told me nothing, ye ye know what I mean? (*She has begun to cry.*)

ALI   Oh don't set me off. Have you got some of this make up?

DENNI   Oh no, I don't want it. De ye know what, that's set up, that – de ye know what I mean, like like keep it from us. That was wrong, that. Why were they a-fucking-shamed about all the

fucking prostitutes and druggies turning up?
That's all the – that's the only life the girl
knew was fucking drugs and prostitution ye
know, she never had no normal friends. So like
people count us as not fucking normal . . .

JILL No one'd give her a condom, ye know? That's
how much she was everyone's mate. She used
to live with me, the girl. I kicked off on Julie
because she heard her fuckin' alarm going and
did fuck-all about it. That girl was old school.
See, there's no 'all for one an' one for all' now,
it's 'all for me' – there used to be – but then it
all went kaput, didn't it? 'Cause of the crack
and the fuckin' heroin and all that.

DENNI (*unclear*) Ye know I am, I can't bear it. I can't
bear it.

ALI Ye know what I mean, she found her. (*To*
ANDY.) She needs help, mate. She found her
body, yeh. (*To* DENNI.) Sorry babes.

JILL What are ye saying sorry for? What are ye
saying sorry for? Shut up, I'll punch your
fuckin' head in.

ALI Fuckin' won't.

JILL Twat. (*To outreach worker.*) Talking like you
know it all. Fuckin' jumped up woolly-back.

DENNI (*tearfully*) Where's me beer? Where's me beer?

JILL Come on baby, we're going. (*Aggressively, to
audience.*) More upset we get, better it is for
you, isn't it? (*Over her shoulder to somebody.*)
You – fuck off.

(*To audience, blisteringly.*) I'm exactly the
same as you. Ye get some smack-head's who
are like, "Ah today's this, and this is my little
bubble", but I'm not like that. I think about
today, think about tomorrow, think about a

week's time, think about me family, plan, save.
I'm exactly the same as you, the only thing is
instead of going on make-up and facials and
that, I rub and dry. That's the only difference
between me and you. Ye might not like it but it
is. It's the only difference.

(*The girls exit in different directions, leaving
the outreach workers to tidy up.*)

Scene Two

LEE *and* LUCY

LEE

I hate that term professional, I really do, 'cause
to me, anyone who's learnt something – you're
a professional, carpenter's a professional,
y'know? Basically left the army after seven
years. Which I'd always wanted to do – that or
play for Everton, like. It was, what am I gonna
do now? I wanted to do drugs work basically.
Grew up 1980, 79-80, when the gear – when the
gear first came round here. A lot of mates got
into it.

LUCY

Crack was just starting to, to come out as well,
you know. They wanted someone to, to go out
there and find out what was, what was going
on, erm, it was a bit sorta' like dirty research
really, you know? Crack's had a terrible impact
on this city. Crack use does make people very
much, you know, like paranoid schizophrenics
with attitude. So they will do more desperate
acts, you know. Crack was very, very cleverly
marketed, erm, across the country and people
were kind of sucked into it. Now, you can't
really buy heroin on its own. You know you've
got to buy the two. It's either two white and a
brown, or two brown and a white you know,
but whatever way, they're getting crack when
they go . . . Erm, so I'd sit in crack houses and
shooting galleries, I'd be climbing in through
windows to places. When I think now I think,

God, how did I get away with that? You know it was madness.

ALI   Lucy Marsh . . . she's worked voluntary for years, honestly she's unreal . . .

LUCY   I can remember the first time I met Ali, she was standing on the corner of Faulkner Street and I went, "I'm just your friendly neighbourhood outreach worker, if you need any needles and syringes I've got all kinds in my boot you know." Once they saw me talking to one, they all started coming down 'cause they're terribly nosy as well. And that's a good quality for an outreach worker, is being nosy, I have to say. And the vice squad came and they were like, "Who's she?" 'Cause they thought I was a new working girl, he said, "Have you got any condoms for us?" And I said, "Sorry I don't stock any in extra small," and the women were like, (*Laughing, mocking noise.*) "Aghhh," sort of thing. So I got to know them. Women were just starting to go out because of their drug problems. What's unfortunate is now they're in an even worse mess than what they were when I first went out there.

ALI   Liverpool was the pioneers, right, in giving out clean syringes, clean condoms, outreach workers, blah, blah. D'you know now, Liverpool, right, has got the worst reputation for drugs services, for Hepatitis, for girls losing legs, for girls with all kinds sexually transmitted diseases?

LUCY   In those days it was a lot easier because there wasn't all this funding problems you've got now to get people in rehab. Thanks to Margaret Thatcher you know, erm, things all changed you know. I mean that woman's got a lot to answer for, you know. There was women coming out to pay their poll tax. Oh, Margaret Thatcher put a lot of women on the game, that woman did. She'll burn in hell when she dies. (*She laughs.*) I hate her.

ALI   Outreach work was going for a long time and then they stopped. Now they've started going out again and they're seeing the damage that had happened in them ten years they stopped. I was in a taxi with this taxi driver I've known for a long time, and he said to me, "Ali, do you know what? I've known girls for years" . . . he's worked in that area for years . . . "A girl got in this cab the other day, she said to me, "I'll give you sex without a condom to take me for a three pound fare." And you think, most of them are injecting, right? Eighty – more than eighty percent of injectors have got Hepatitis C. Now if they're doing it – sex without – they take it back to their wives. It's a vicious circle, that is, a vicious circle.

LEE   A lot of people say, "What's ye su" – mates – "Oh what's ye success rate?" If ye measuring success on getting someone clean, over seven years of doing this job, probably not even, ye know, not even half a percent. If ye looking at changing lives as in, someone was using a lot of drugs and now they're just using the script. That's a big difference, ye know.

LUCY   It was about stopping the damage that people were actually doing to themselves, you know? Their legs would be swollen: deep vein thrombosis of the legs. You'd see them, you'd go, "Hang on, you need to get in." The first thing the women asked me was, "Are you a social worker?" and I'd go, "No I haven't even got an O-Level, love." (*Laughs.*)

ALI   I came out of school with eleven O-Levels. I could have done something.

LUCY   And I always gave them two choices because they'd be quite resistant to go to hospital, I'd say, "Look you've got two choices, either you

get in the car and I take you to hospital, or I
knock you out (*Laughs*.) and I'll take you
anyway!" And they'd usually take the first
one. Sometimes you have to take control, you
know. (*Pause*.) The police overstep the mark
loads of times. I've seen a plain-clothes officer
threaten to kill one of the girls and said no
one'd know. She'd just walked out of a pub and
he was deciding to harass her. And all the
heavy policing did, like Operation Angel, is
they've spread it to a much wider area so it's
costing in effect more money and it's driven it
further underground so you can't reach the
women. (*Beat*.) I'm ambivalent about the zone.

LEE   I don't think it's been really cleared up
            properly.

(ANDY *has come up*.)

ANDY   Y'know if a life is lost, it's lost and can't be
            repaired . . . If you look at the two murders that
            lead to the big debate about zoning three years
            ago. Those women went back to the man's flat.
            If you had a zone, you wouldn't risk going
            back to a punter's place.

LUCY   I am a bit concerned whether that would be like
            putting them into a cattle market. And then
            what would their safety be when they're
            coming out of the zone? I'd like to see it de-
            criminalised so that women have more choices
            in the way that they operate, and to make it
            more safe. CCTV.

ANDY   People confuse zoning and legalisation of
            brothels. Right? Very concerned and
            empathetic people say the women should be
            given places to work and we should legalise
            brothels and they'll work indoors. (*Sighs*.)
            Misunderstands the indoor industry, most
            indoor premises will not allow heavily addicted
            women, most heavily addicted women couldn't
            work the shifts, wouldn't want the commitment

of long shifts. Why people are in street sex work, they've gotta remember is because of the flexibility it gives. It's about survival, they've got chaotic lives, girls will walk around with their life in like a carrier bag . . .

LEE   Ye get people: "Oh there's a meeting tonight." "What for?" "Oh about the managed zone." "Oh, I didn't know nothing about it." "Yeh we're all going, yeh we wanna be in on the ground level on this," and ye thinking oh my God, because it's a good little subject for people to sit around the dinner table? (*Pause.*) I think drug workers come in two categories. There are those who are the realists, and those who are living complete la-la land where they think they – they're gonna change the world.

ALI   I hate it when patronising drugs counsellors, right? Text book druggies I call them. "Ali, I know how you feel. Really terrible. These withdrawal feelings that you go through . . ." And I go, "Why? What was you on?" "Well nothing, I read it, you know . . ." You can't tell me you know what a rattle's like. So don't. Just go and get me script. And I don't need fifty mls, I need eighty. Do you know what they are? (*Putting on a deep dramatic voice.*) The Crusaders. They do my fucking head in.

LEE   I ain't in it for that game. I'm in it, to be honest, because what started out to be you know, an altruistic ideal, I suppose it's now a case of I have to earn dough to pay me mortgage an all that. (*He goes.*)

ALI   I'd like to go back to when I went to school, right? Do you know when they go into schools and they go, "Heroin is bad," well I'd like to go in and go, "Heroin isn't bad, first time you have it, you're gonna love it.' I wanna say, "Listen, you're gonna love it. That'll be for weeks. But do you know after a while?" . . . and then tell them my story.

(PAT *has sat back down in her chair with a cup of tea.*)

PAT So, er . . . (*Sighs.*) Where am I up to . . . where am I up to . . . I thought, I've got no qualms with this Rob Fairwell. I had no worries about him at all. I thought, this is really gonna work. This is good. (*She smiles.*) They moved to Southport. She used to bring the baby down every fortnight . . . depended on the mood she was in, 'cause I . . . well, we had our ups and downs me and Pauline, yer know? I'd say it was a clash of personalities. We were too much alike. But we still loved each other. (*Pause.*) Anyway, we were in the pub one night and Pauline comes running in, "Mum, can you lend me a tenner? I'll give it yer back tomorrow." I went, "Okay. 'Ere ye are." And as I turned round I seen Rob Fairwell. And I went, "Jesus Christ! What happened to you?" "I've got a bad back." And I thought "Yer alright, mate. Y've got a bad back. 'Cause I've had a bad back for thirty years I don't look like you." (*Pause.*) He was – honest to God – it'd take yer a week to walk round this man, he was so big, and when I seen him he must have been nine and a half stone – the weight loss was just dramatic. And I went, no, not again, I can't be doing with this. Not again. And I was screamin' at him in the pub, "Yer lying bastard! Yer liar! Yer a liar! Yer on the fuckin gear! Yer on the gear and yer've got me daughter back on the gear!" I just lost it – and I beat the crap out of him. I did. And Pauline's screamin' at me and I went, "I don't care Pauline, yer not telling me that he's got a bad back. I'm not stupid anymore."

ALI You've gotta be honest with kids. Telling them it's bad, it's evil? It doesn't work.

PAT He lost his job. Lost his house. They ended up living in Skem.

LUCY	They're out there to support their habits. The big survey I did in 2002: ninety-five percent were heroin and crack users. The drugs fill a big hole in their lives.
ALI	I could not go out there normal.
LUCY	I always remember one lad that I was working with and erm, he said, when he took heroin, "I felt as if I was in cotton wool and somebody was just holding me . . ."
ALI	I'm telling you now, you'll get a warm glow, makes you feel good, you feel confident . . . but at the end of the day . . . like me . . . I'm on a lead and a collar now. I can't go away for two weeks. I can't go away for the weekend. I can go that far and it pulls me back. That far and it pulls me back.
PAT	If I could've bullied Pauline into stoppin' what she was doin', by Christ I would've done. I'd've locked her up and thrown away the key. (*Little pause.*) But once they turn eighteen . . . they're on their own.
ALI	I mean I'll tell them the good but I'll tell them the fucking bad.

(*She comes forward.*)

Scene Three

Ali's Story

ALI	I was in the wrong place, wrong time. Very small – you know? Small petite girl. He'd tried to get two girls in before me. Picked me, put me in the car, started towards the Albert Dock. I'm at the lights and he's already gone, "Ee are, here's your money". So seems trustworthy to me, you know? Hair all back, business, tie,

suit, the lot. And he said to me – we're at the
lights and the lights are changing – and he said
to me, "Just grab that wheel and I'll put me foot
down and turn the corner" . . . and as I did . . .
handcuffs on. (*Pause*.) Took me to a house that
he owned, he was renting out to students. The
students had gone back for the summer, right?
A chain through the handcuffs and a knife in
me back, taking me up the stairs. I'm on the
third floor. Then it was, em, sitting in a hard
back chair in the middle of the room and there
was a big window there and he was a big fella.
Grey hair . . . took all me clothes off, with the
knife, with the knife. . . . "Do you know what
you are? You're the devil's spawn, just a dirty
prostitute. Now get on your knees and say
sorry to God for what yer are." So I started to
– I realised if I argued with him I was making
him angrier and it was getting worse, it was
going up and up in scale. So I had to play him
– and I was like, "Sorry God", but then he
boots me. Burnt a cross in me back. I had
seventeen crosses burnt in me back off him.
"That wasn't sincere enough. Do it again."
Raped me three times. And then he went dead
calm. Got out a bottle of whisky, gave me a
drink, he's got the other chair and he's sitting
facing me now. I'm shaking and he's, "Calm
down, you're alright. Here's a cigarette, here's
some whisky." And I'm like "Wow. What's
happening here?" And he said, "Now you're
going to have to listen to me Ali." He turned me
head up, took my hand . . . I'll never forget his
eyes – my jaw was shattered, my nose was
gone, I mean I was in a really bad way – he said
"You've seen my face and you'll be able to
identify me so I'm going to have to kill you.
(*Pause*.) I'm going into that kitchen to get the
knife to kill you." And I thought, "Well before
you kill me mate, I'll kill myself." (*Quietly*.) I'll
kill myself. (*Pause*.) Jumped out the window,
three floors up and landed. Me ankles
shattered. Taxi driver was going past, picked
me up, wrapped me in his coat . . . All the

bizzies meet up and here he is coming out the chippie with a meal. (*Pause.*) I was in hospital, couldn't speak for eleven days. Twelve hours that man tortured me. He went, "not guilty" and the crown court took the trial all the way. Made me re-live the whole experience again. And they just said, because he'd been in the army, because he'd lost his job and was losing his house . . . he'd suffered enough. (*Pause.*) And if I was a normal woman he would be receiving fifteen years in prison. Because I'm a prostitute . . . it's the 'hazards of the job'. He got an eighteen month suspended sentence and his driving licence took off him. (*Pause.*) Know what I think? I think he'd had a bad time with his mum!

After I got kidnapped . . . they didn't know nothing about it. It was on the front page of the *Echo*, it'd been to court . . . and it said my name like, so I had to ring my mum and tell her . . . she just said, "Get a taxi". All's I was worried about was me mum, me mums friends, me dads friends. They're respected. And I just felt so dirty and horrible. (*Pause.*) Me mum just had hold of me and . . . that night they made me go out and have a drink with them in the club that they've drank in for years, so they could go . . . "This is our daughter".

Scene Four

The Government's Response

A GOVERNMENT OFFICIAL *in a suit is coming forward, shuffling papers in preparation to speak.*

ANDY   (*has opened a copy of* The Guardian, *reads aloud from it*) The government will announce plans next month for a national zero tolerance campaign against . . .

GOVT OFFICIAL   (*overlapping simultaneously*) . . . kerb crawlers and street prostitution after shelving plans to allow red-light 'toleration zones'.

(ANDY *throws the paper down.*)

ALI   (*on her phone*) You are fuckin' joking me. Aw – that's terrible. (*Beat.*) And did you have a nice birthday, babes?

GOVT OFFICIAL   The government will make proposals for an amendment to the definition of a brothel so that two or three individuals may work together.

ALI   . . . I'm gonna have to call you later . . . I've just had the nod. Yeah. He's indicating and turning round. See ya babes.

DIANE   Well I phoned them up last night 'cause I was so mad. I said what about the sixty percent that are homeless? How can they run a brothel if they're on the streets? You're taking them off the streets because people are making big complaints about them walking in front of people's houses, so you're gonna stick them next door to someone and have a brothel running?

GOVT OFFICIAL   We are not trying, by having a clear strategy in the street sex market, to move it from the streets to a series of pairs of women working out of flats and causing a nuisance. The clear aim of the government will be to disrupt street sex markets to significantly reduce the numbers involved in street prostitution.

DIANE   Three girls to each house? So how many brothels does that take in Liverpool?

GOVT OFFICIAL   The creation of a managed area, even as a short term arrangement, could give the impression that communities condone, or at least are forced to accept, street prostitution and the exploitation of women.

ANDY
Managed areas don't condone, they're simply practical intervention that allow you to work more effectively keeping people alive.

CATHERINE
Our managed zone would have given girls access to drug treatment and help to exit prostitution. We have to work with prostitutes rather than arrest them or their clients.

GOVT OFFICIAL
It is a form of child abuse. Most women who are prostitutes started being prostitutes at the age of thirteen or fourteen and we have got to have strong mechanisms to reduce prostitution. Prostitution blights communities. We will take a zero tolerance approach to kerb crawling. Men who use prostitutes are indirectly supporting drug dealers and abusers. Effective policing, rather than an overhaul of the laws, is the answer.

(*The* GOVT OFFICIAL *leaves.*)

ANDY
Right, where to start? The frame that they've gone for is one of exploitation isn't it? They've gone with this statement that we cannot tolerate prostitution, it's not acceptable. To me that doesn't enhance the rights of sex workers. Street sex workers remain criminalised, so that puts a real block on the supposed objectives that the government want to achieve which is accessing them into services, yeah?

DIANE
They're sitting up there in their cosy little offices – I was so annoyed last night I nearly got on the train and went to London. I wanted to speak to whassername, Fiona McTaggart.

ANDY
It's going to have an absolutely devastating impact. With a crackdown on clients, the result will be an increase in criminalisation and an increase in rape and other violence. That's

what we have seen every previous time that has been put forward. Women work later, take more risks. Still people will risk getting murdered.

CATHERINE People say to you in politics, never, never put your head above the parapet. Well there are times when you have to. And this is one of those times.

ANDY This is people selling sex. Let's face it, this is what's rarely said – we're not good at talking about sex. It's really difficult for some people but all I would say is, it's happening. And it's happening down scabby stairs and dirty alleyways. Where people are at risk. Zero tolerance won't protect the most vulnerable women and won't stop them working. It will drive them underground and put their lives at risk.

CATHERINE We will now tell the government that we do not want a change in the law, we just want to hold a three year pilot. No one has tackled prostitution in this way before, so they cannot say it will definitely fail.

DIANE Last night I thought, well they're just trying to shut me up but it's not gonna work. They won't shut me up until I get what I want.

CATHERINE Unprotected, that is what the girls will be – that is what our communities will be. How do you have zero tolerance when there are not enough police officers to cover every street, twenty four hours a day? How do girls protect themselves when making instant decisions about punters? That is what zero tolerance forces girls to do. The drug issues won't have vanished overnight, so girls will keep working as the problem shifts from neighbourhood to neighbourhood. We need measures that will work to solve this problem, not sound bites!

(*The meeting dissolves.*)

ALI (*on her own now*) Here's the tree now. Here's the tree now. There must be at least, what? Twenty, bunches of . . . with cards, with thingies written on. This is where she was left like a fuckin' rag doll. Ooh, d'you know what, honest to God I can't even look at it. Fucking hell, when are people gonna realise that we're fucking people. You tell me what I am doing wrong on this street that deserves something like that!

(*Fade in a soundscape of genuine footage of girls' voices.*)

GIRLS' VOICE OVERS "I got me throat cut and attempted murder on me – Hanane Parry who got murdered and found in bin bags last year, she got murdered, she went missing from my house . . . /It was 8 o'clock tonight, erm, I picked a guy up and took him down, erm, where they take 'em right and that that, er, he tried to rape me . . . /If you're going into a hotel it's forty quid, twenty five for sex, fifteen for a suck and it's ten for a hand-job. I've got no other way of fundin' me habit, I can't shoplift, I'm like a bag o' nerves so the only thing I can do is sell myself . . . / I've been smoking crack and if I wasn't doing heroin I wouldn't be out on the streets. If there's one thing I want to do it's . . . get off the drugs . . . (*She weeps.*) . . . I am I just . . . wanna get off them (*A long, pained cry.*) . . . fuckin' hell it's . . . they're doing me fucking head in . . ." (*She weeps.*)

(ALI *is with* DIANE *at a café table.*)

DIANE Her teacher come up to me and she goes, "I didn't want to give you this 'cause I thought it might upset" – "No no I can handle anything" – so anyway I put this video on. I couldn't even breathe, I couldn't even speak. Because, she was real on this. I know Hanane was real

ACT TWO

anyway but sometimes you're looking at a picture and it just catches the moment doesn't it? This, this . . . and she's like a little doll, a porcelain doll, and she had all her hair tied back and she was just sitting, er, this like, erm, swing thing . . . she's just sitting there and, erm, all these, erm, all her friends are on the swings and that and she's just sitting there in a world of her own and caught her and I was going – it upset me because even then, even before she was just in this little world of her own . . .

(*Beat*.)

My liason officer had to warn me before we went into court that they would use . . . name her as a prostitute.

ALI   Not just prostitute, common prostitute.

DIANE   But now . . . like if I go to somebody – if I go – I say, "She was working the streets, because she was a heroin addict."

ALI   Doing a job./

DIANE   /Yeh.

ALI   Just like anyone else. Except it's a bit of a, a horizontal position job, that's all as I say. (*They laugh*.) Mary Magdelene was a prostitute.

DIANE   Who?

ALI   The one that washed Jesus's feet was a prostitute.

DIANE   Oh my God.

ALI   So any time anyone says that, just say, "Mary Magdelene was a prostitute." My mother tells everyone that.

DIANE   Oh does she?

ALI   You know Hanane, her name, does that mean
             anything?

DIANE   Kindness. And she gives everything in her life
             away. (*Pause*.) Nineteen going on for a little
             girl. (*Beat*.) And they give me this five
             thousand pounds. It made me physically sick.

ALI   Blood money.

DIANE   Me mum always said . . . "Never make a God
             out of money." So I bought everybody keep-
             sake things, just threw all the money away.
             (*Beat*.) But the lady that deals with the girls/

ALI   /Outreach worker.

DIANE   Said, "Get em a bit of lippy." So I go in the
             chemist and there's all these lipsticks reduced
             and I went, "I'll 'ave the lot." She goes, "What
             on earth are you buying all those lipsticks
             for?" I said –/

ALI   /Prostitutes.

DIANE   Prostitutes! Her face is an absolute picture. I
             went to Marks and Spencer's. I said, "I've
             three hundred and forty pounds for knickers
             socks and gloves. Because at the end of the
             day – they don't deserve to wear people's
             second-hand underwear." So this woman said,
             "Marks and Spencer's have charities of their
             own, but we can sort something out." They
             never got in touch with me again ever. I hate
             Marks and Spencer's now.

ALI   Go to George at Asda.

DIANE   I went to Woollies. The manager said, "Every
             two pairs of knickers you buy, we'll throw a
             third free." So me and me friend went round
             with this trolley, it was full, packed with socks,
             knickers, the lot. I tell you, we had a right
             laugh, there, with all that stuff.

ALI   You didn't get them big fat Sloggis and that,
            did you?

DIANE   They're all quite skinny, aren't they, cause
            most of them are on drugs.

            (*Pause.*)

ALI   When was the last time you seen her, before?

DIANE   Two years before she was murdered.

ALI   You're joking.

DIANE   I spoke to her . . . all the time on the phone.

            (*Lights fade on* ALI *and* DIANE. BRIAN *comes
            forward.*)

BRIAN   Hanane, erm, yeh, I'd picked her up a few
            times. But she went down, down, down. She
            was living with two people who both had bad
            habits who wouldn't work the streets. So she
            was scoring for the three of them, ye know
            what I mean? But she was out continuously
            that girl, rain, hail, shine. I picked her up maybe
            three or four times. But she was . . . She was
            sad, ye know. (*Pause.*) Some girls thee get in
            the car, they're bubbly, they're doing what
            they're doing. Don't, don't get me in the car
            and yer sad and I feel as if I'm abusing yer and
            I, I, that was what I felt . . . 'This person is so
            sad man. She's, she's, she's sad.'

            (*He leaves. Beat.*)

DIANE   There's part of me that does feel the guilt – I
            should have brought her home.

ALI   Believe me, it wouldn't have made any
            difference, I'm telling you now.

DIANE Yeh but the thing is erm, how can I say this? Is she was like, erm . . . nobody reported her missing.

ALI 'Cause that's because you hadn't seen her though.

DIANE I'll never know her last words. That's haunted me, you know, like –

ALI Yeh I know what you're saying there, like. But don't you think you're better off not knowing that?

DIANE But I want to.

ALI But it'd haunt you worse if you knew it.

DIANE No but I should have brought her home, shouldn't I?

ALI No.

DIANE Yeh I know but, it's like as if she didn't exist there was this, there was this body. (*Crying.*) She should have come home.

ALI That's wrong, honestly. My mum took me home and took me home, and I was still sneaking out, getting dressed in little skirts, sneaking out of the window. It could have been me dying. My mum didn't know.

DIANE She wanted to come home though. I wouldn't let her.

(*She cries.*)

Scene Five

PAT I knew she was back on the streets. There's nothing I could have done about it. (*Beat.*) Next thing, our Margaret rings me . . . "Have yer heard from Pauline?" I said, "No, I haven't heard nothin'." She said, "Mum, somethin's not right." "What do yer mean, somethin's not right? She's probably just been arrested." She said, "No, I've rang all the police stations . . . I've rang the hospitals . . . somethin's not right."

DIANE Hanane phoned me up a week before he'd murdered her, and I was watering the garden, the grass in the back 'coz we'd just had grass put down. And we had a good laugh on the phone and I said about Alex, her friend, had had a baby, and then she said, "I got to go now."

PAT We gave it till the Monday. No sign. So we rings the local bobbies. They came round. Had a look round the house, make sure she wasn't here, which they had to do. And . . . they went away. That was on the Monday. On the Wednesday the serious crimes came up. Debbie, Rob and Tom . . . they said because Pauline'd just sort of disappeared . . . they were really quite worried about her. (*Little pause.*) Well, by this time me nerves had gone. I thought, there's somethin', somethin' not right here. Somethin's goin' on. Erm, that was on the Wednesday. (*Little pause.*) They came out every day . . . the police . . . askin' me little, little questions. On the Sunday . . . the police came to say that they'd found some clothin' that was similar to Pauline's and I knew then. I knew then. He said, "I need to prepare you. Now. That if I've got to come back later and tell you that it is Pauline, I don't want it to be a complete shock." And I went, "I know she's dead. I know. In my heart I know she's dead." So. Twenty past eight on the Sunday night . . . they came . . . they walked in and they just said, "We're sorry Pat. We've found body parts."

(PAT *begins to cry – quietly.* BILLY *rises from sofa/chair, brings over the box of tissues.* PAT *takes a couple, dabs her eyes, her nose.*)

DIANE   They were looking for Pauline, the other girl. But nobody reported Hanane missing. She'd been dead for like nine days. The body was decomposed and chopped into pieces, and half of it was taken to Stanley Park, and the other half dumped in bin bags.

PAT   They asked . . . they asked me . . . if there was anythin' distinguishin' about Pauline. And I said, "Yeah, long blonde hair, right down her back." Anythin' else?

DIANE   They knew she was mixed race. That's all they knew about her.

PAT   "A tattoo . . . on her arm . . . two hearts entwined." And then they asked about jewellery . . . she had my engagement ring . . . and this thing with a cross on. Did she smoke? And I said, "Yeah. Rollies. But she put them into a ten box of Lambert and Butler." (*Little pause.*) And he said, "I'm sorry Pat." He said, "We can confirm that it's Pauline." (*She breaks down again. Pause.*)

DIANE   Roy come in and he said, "I've got to tell your Mummy something. Now, you go outside with your friend and play." And probably I was already crying, 'cause I knew what was coming. I was sick, and I wet myself. I'm not embarrassed to say that. I must have gone on auto pilot, 'cause I can't even remember half of what I did. Roy said, "You've booked this holiday," he said, "Get away because," he said "I'm telling you now . . ." The press had hounded them. They wanted a picture, they wanted a name. Roy said, er, "Ye'll have to tell your friends, your family, and, er, and the children within an hour." Well you can imagine what it was like. Who the hell – How the hell do I do all this without offending somebody in one hour? I thought, where do I start? So, erm, I said to Roy, "How do I do it? How do I tell the kids?" He goes, "I don't know." He said, "I've been a liaison officer, and police officer for so many years," he said, "but we've never dealt with a murder quite as horrific as this." And I went, oh, in other words, in me own head, I had to get up and get on with it.

PAT   Apparently I went nuts in here . . . but I don't remember it. Erm . . . me dad rang round for Billy and Michael, and, er, they come running round. Screaming at them – Douglas went out and broke both his arms by hitting the walls. (*Little pause.*)

DIANE   I wasn't conscious that I was . . . I was sitting there scraping me legs and me fingernails. I've got that much pain on the inside, I want to feel it on the outside, literally, feel it physically.

PAT   Having to tell an eight year old boy that his mum was dead, was the worst thing in my life I've had to do and . . . I'll never forget it.

DIANE   So I had to take them one at a time in the garden and tell 'em. They knew that she was a heroin addict, so she could come home and she could still have her friends in this . . . you know, in Broughton. And they'd support her with her heroin addiction and she could even get a flat around here. But I didn't want Hanane to be called . . . come back and be called a slapper and everything else. So I kept it from everybody. Even John had a go at me 'coz he said, "If you'd have told me I would have gone and picked her up." He didn't know, I didn't tell anybody. Nobody. It was like a secret life. Next thing, on the telly, Hanane's face, name, prostitute.

PAT   I sat him down and I told him that the naughty man had come and his Mum was dead. Two days later he come screaming in here to me, "I know how my mum died, I know how my mum died. She was chopped in bits." All the kids outside. Taking the mick out of him. "Your mum was chopped up." So I had to sit him back down again and tell him again that it didn't really matter, because the angels had already come and took ye mum, and she didn't feel nothing. My dog, Tyson, came down the stairs, walked into the living room and put his head on James's knee, as if to say, "I'm here. I understand."

DIANE   All that night I literally sat down crying . . . I couldn't go to bed because every time I went to bed and closed my eyes I had this picture of him strangling me, now I didn't know that she'd been strangled, but I had this picture – every time I went to sle – closed my eyes – I woke up like that 'cause he was round my neck. The thing's that'd be going through my head that he'd tortured her and slashed her while she was alive.

PAT   (*little pause*) The first week was just a blur. I had a lot of people here. The media. It was . . . to be honest it was just a nightmare.

DIANE   They put me on valium for three days and I was on that settee and I couldn't even function half the time . . . I was taking pain killers and eventually I just said to Wendy, I need to sleep, I need to sleep, so uh, I fell asleep for about two seconds on the settee there and I woke up and I went who's that man and Wendy goes what man, there's no man in here, I said that man standing there in the black shirt. God knows what I was doing, I don't know what planet I was on . . . I was hysterical all night. And do you know the woman that, uhm, like you phone the emergency doctor up and a woman comes on the phone doesn't she and, uh, she goes off and gets the doctor . . . and she said, uh, oh, you can't speak to the doctor, she said, but talk to me, she said . . . she said talk to me if you want to talk to somebody. She said where are you? I said . . . I had all the lights off in the house . . . I said I'm sitting down here in the dark, on the floor and I can't breathe . . .

(*Little pause.*)

PAT

On the Tuesday after she was found . . . They had a suspect. (*Little pause.*) So . . . they went and raided his flat . . . and that's where they found (*Long pause.* PAT *lights up a cigarette – her hands are shaking.*) He'd gone to the shop two days before and bought the stuff that he needed. The hacksaw.

DIANE

I said, "Was she wearing clothes?" Apparently he stripped her. She was ready to leave the flat. And, erm, he strangled her, stripped her, and then cut her up. In that order apparently. But, erm, I said, "Well, was she found with any clothes?" and Roy said, "No." and I said, I told Roy to go to the coroner, I said, "I don't want all these men gawping at her." I said, "Even though she's dead and in bits." I said, "I said I don't want all these men gawping at her 'cause she's got no clothes on."

PAT

The police were brilliant. Liaison officers. I can't fault them. (*Little Pause.*) They did everythin' they could for me. But something like this – they said that she was probably strangled. They don't know. Because of the injuries they can't – it's unascertained how she died. (*Pause.*) I still believe that the psychic was right . . . she died from a blow to the back of the head . . . and that she fought for an hour and a half. I still believe that. She . . . she'd've battled. She would've put up a fight. (*Little pause.*) She could handle herself. I brought her up that way.

DIANE   She had to be sent in a sealed body bag
          wrapped in a sheet . . . Funeral director comes
          to me mum's and he goes have you got any
          special clothes, uhm, that you want to dress
          her in and I went get real and he goes what do
          you mean. And I said, "Listen, she's in
          bleeding bits." I said, "How the fuck can you
          dress someone if they're in bits?" (*Pause.*) I
          said to Roy, before I went to the funeral, what
          if I cry too much. He went, what a strange
          question. He said, "You won't." "What if I
          don't cry at all?" I was scared in case I didn't
          cry at all, I was scared in case I collapsed, cried
          too much . . . I've never buried anyone before
          . . . I never been to me nan's funeral . . . I've
          only been to the service 'coz I couldn't stand
          anyone going into the hole. It didn't really hit
          me till I seen the coffin and then I went
          hysterical. (*Pause.*) I'm glad in the end that I
          didn't have her buried. I'm glad I had her
          cremated in the end because she was back in
          one piece, wasn't she? He didn't have that
          hold over her any more.

PAT   But if he'd just strangled her and left her like
          that, at least I'd have been able to see her. But
          to do that . . . (*Sniffs.*) To chop her up and put
          her in bin bags. And leave her head in the
          freezer. No . . . can't do it.

          (*Pause while she cries.* KEVIN *comes forward.*)

Epilogue

KEVIN   (*reading an official statement*) The
          dismembered bodies of Hanane Parry, ninteen,
          and Pauline Stephen, twenty-five, were found
          in the red light district of St Domingo Vale in
          July, 2003. (*He reads from a second piece of
          paper.*) September, 2005. The body of Anne
          Marie Foy was found in Crown Street near the
          Royal Liverpool Hospital. A post-mortem

revealed that she was badly beaten and there was evidence of strangulation.

(ANNE MARIE'S *voice is heard on tape, over.*)

ANNE MARIE (VO)   "You're never safe. Ye know out there, ye – it's it's – it is – like every every car you get into ye don't know whether ye gonna get out of it. It's it's dangerous all the time, ye don't realise how dangerous. And me of all people do realise 'cos I have been in situations where I've nearly died."

(*A projection shows the dates of* ANNE MARIE'S *life.* ALI *comes forward.*)

ALI   It could be anyone's daughter, I know but . . . people don't see it like that. You're just dirt to them. (*Pause.*) My dad said . . . he never mentioned it till he was dying . . . he said . . . "Listen. I've never spoke to you about it but . . . you never changed in my eyes." That's all I needed to hear from him, do you know what I mean? It killed me, but I really needed to hear it from him.

(*Lights fade.*)